M000267013

The Voice Positioning System™

7 Ways to Harness Your Power and Master Your Influence

Dr. Katrina Hutchins

The Voice Positioning System™:
7 Ways to Harness Your Power and Master Your Influence

Copyright © 2018 Dr. Katrina Hutchins
All rights reserved.

Published by Re-Source Solutions, LLC
Photo Credit: Denise Benson Photography
Cover Design: Langley D. Shealy

No portion of this publication may be reproduced, stored in a retrieval system or transmitted in any form by any means – electronic, mechanical, photocopying, screenshot, recording, or any other – except for brief quotations in printed reviews, without the prior written permission of the author.

ISBN: 978-1-68111-262-6

Printed in the United States of America

0   1   2   3   4   5   6

To Mom – for bringing my voice to life.

I also dedicate this book to the women who were a part of my research study and who freely and courageously gave their voices to this work and to those I have met along the way who are positioning their voices in powerful ways.

DID YOU KNOW...

Only 7% of your VOICE is communicated through words.
The question is...
How are you positioning your 93%?

CONTENTS

PROLOGUE

Upon my first encounter with Dr. Katrina Hutchins (Dr. K), there was a deep knowing in my spirit that there would be something more to come in our future. There are those times when there is no denying that a connection is divinely appointed, and this was undeniably just that. Then, after having the immense pleasure of sitting in the audience while she spoke, it solidified that inner knowing even further.

Fast forward a few months and a few dialogues later, Dr. K asked if I would do her the honor of writing the foreword for this dynamic breadth of work. There was no other answer but–YES. I heard the answer spring forth from my cells, in the form of a huge smile before the verbal communication left my lips.

As I had the pleasure of reading through the chapters of this amazing book, I could literally see myself in many of the scenarios and circumstances mentioned. There was a moment of freedom as I realized I now had a term to connect with my experiences - organizational silence; WOW.

Throughout my professional climb, there were instances where I experienced blatant inappropriateness, yet I looked the other way. I would also show up in a space inauthentic to the very person I was. However, I experienced a fear of what would happen if I brought my voice forward or positioned myself against the "others". I remember battling with my inner voice.

Herein lies the cyclical self-bantering that can and will destroy you from the inside out, if you allow it. What I know for sure is that your inner empire must have its queen in command of the throne. If we look at history, any successful kingdom has their engaged and committed leader. You too must show up as that committed individual to yourself, your vision, your dreams, your ideas and even stand in the gap for others as the leader.

This is why The Voice Positioning System is a crucial piece of literature for us to not only read, but to practice. The act of repetition will allow the words of this book to become integrated into your daily acts, which will then create a different result in your life. This book will not only grow you as a leader in your professional life, it will also contribute immensely to the growth in your personal life.

Had a book of this caliber been available in the beginning of my leadership journey, I know I would not have experienced so many hard knocks. Dr. K has begun a movement, and I am completely on board.

Alycia Huston
CEO & Founder
LeadHERship Adventures, LLC

PREFACE

In 2013, I began my doctoral studies at Northeastern University. While extremely excited to be pursing my degree, I was not exactly certain about the focus of my research. I was certain, however, about my interest in studying women in organizations. With this interest leading the way, I immersed myself in literature and research studies related to organizational theory and organizational behavior. I read, and I read, and then I read some more. Then it happened! In exploring the depth and breadth of the literature, I happened upon a phenomenon that was notably prevalent in organizations of all types, a phenomenon termed as *organizational silence.*

The choice not to speak up, but rather to remain silent or withhold opinions and ideas about issues or concerns at work, is within itself the most simplistic description of organizational silence. This form of silence comprises thoughts that are never shared, ideas that are never heard, conversations that are never had, and an overall avoidance of speaking up; even when speaking up could bring about positive change. In other words, organizational silence represents a population of people, who for various reasons, show up for work daily, and yet they are silent, silenced, or both.

Here it was in the literature right in front of me. The definitions from scholars and years of research studies on organizational silence seemed to leap off the pages and form the proverbial light bulb over my head. In black and white, here was the language for my own experiences in organizations - experiences I had not been able to assign words to. It was just a feeling; an indescribable feeling. It was here that the research became personal. I wanted to understand more about this phenomenon of organizational silence. I wanted to understand what happened, how it happened, and why it happened. But more than anything else, I wanted to understand its impact on women–not just in the workplace; but also, in their life. I wanted to understand their experiences of silence and what it meant for them to exist in that state of being at work.

This quest for understanding drove me deeper into the research, only to discover little was known about how women made meaning of silence and how they navigated organizational environments or cultures when they were silent or silenced. My response was, "BINGO! Here is the missing piece from the literature!" My research headed in that direction. I sought to answer the question, *how do women who work in organizations perceive and experience organizational silence in the workplace?*

And The Research Says...

I conducted a qualitative study, which comprised one-on-one interviews with eight phenomenal women who consented to take part in the research. For these eight women in the study, making sense of their lived experiences of silence meant that they would need to assess their silence journeys. In essence, they needed to tell their stories of being silent or silenced at work.

Through sharing their perceptions and experiences of silence in the workplace, each woman honored and validated her *journey into silence,* her *journey in silence,* and/or her *journey out of silence.* Additionally, each woman's unique perceptions and experiences gave *voice* to her diverse journey, whether filled with challenges, triumphs, limitations, courage, failure, and/or resilience; her story illustrated the detriment to our power and influence when we do not enact our authentic voice.

The tables provide a synopsis of the experiences and feelings associated with navigating silence and voice experiences in the workplace. Table 1 represents women who came to the workplace with tendencies toward silence because of prior experiences. Table 2 illustrates the experiences and feelings of women who were silenced after becoming employed in their workplace. Table 3 shows the power of the experiences for the women who embraced their journeys out of silence.

Table 1: Synopsis of Participant Feelings and Experiences When Silent Before Coming to the Workplace

Powerlessness	Apprehension	Submission
Suppression	Pulling Back	Surrender
Hopelessness	Shrinking Back	Self-Muting
Internalized Pain	Self-Minimizing	Loss of Self-Worth
Loss of Confidence	Need to Hide	Self-Doubt
Disenfranchisement	Struggle	Acquiescence to Silence

Table 2: Synopsis of Participant Feelings and Experiences When Silenced After Becoming Employed in the Workplace

Self-Preservation	Resignation	Resentment
Self-protection	Giving Up	Misplaced Voice
Self-silencing	Giving Into	Misplaced Power
Avoidance	Defeat	Rancor
Acquiescence	Emotional Departure	Exasperation
Pulling Back	Embarrassment	Frustration
Invisible	Shame	Undervalued

Table 3: Synopsis of Participant Feelings and Experiences When the Pursuit of Authentic Voice Was Embraced

Self-Regulation	Self-Determination	Self-Inclusion
Control	Resoluteness	Choice
Management	Discernment	Contribution
Responsibility	Voice Commitment	Authenticity

My research study concluded that women's perceptions and experiences of silence were deep-seated and emotional. The study brought to light the impact on personal well-being when women suffer in silence, when they are blinded by silence, and when their authentic voice is trapped under the many masks they wear.

But, most importantly, the study revealed the overwhelming significance of the *power* of women's authentic voices. Specifically, I was able to see and understand the power of *voice* as I had never seen and understood the power of *voice* before. I recognized for many women, the challenge was not in "using" their voices; but rather in "positioning" their voices. So... I wrote a book about it.

What's the Difference?

I was once asked, "What is the difference between your "Brand" and your "Voice"? You may even be wondering that too. I mean after all, there are a plethora of thoughts about building your personal brand. There are steps, strategies, tips, keys, and processes for how to do it successfully. There are programs, books, and courses that will teach ways to develop a good brand.

I am certainly not knocking any aspect of being a brand or building one. However, here is my thought on the difference. Your *Brand* is something you create that exists as a way to define you and what you do. Your *Authentic Voice* is something that was created to live on the inside of you to define who you are. In other words, YOU can create a brand... GOD created your *Authentic Voice*. See the difference?

Now notice I said, *Authentic Voice*. Although I will talk more about this in the *Knowing Your Voice* section of the book, I want to establish the context here.

When I refer to *Authentic Voice*, I am referring to more than just your vocal cords (parts of the physical anatomy that make up voice). When I refer to voice, I am referring to the very essence of who you were created to be. I am referring to your embodiment of God's unique design for you and his purpose and destiny for your life on earth, all rolled-up into your marvelously and wonderfully made self.

When I refer to your Authentic Voice, I am also referring to your unmasked demeanor, your attitude, your disposition, and your character. I am referring to the uninhibited way you enter a room and the way the room feels when you are in it and when you leave it because of your powerful presence. I am referring to the thing that causes others to stop and listen to you, even when you are not speaking.

Words Are Not Everything

Just so we are completely clear, let's talk about your words. While voice is inclusive of words, it is so much more than that. Research shows that only 7% of our communication consists of our words. The other 93% is composed of the language that does not come out of our mouths. This form of communication speaks so much louder than words and holds at its core, our values, our virtues, our character, and our qualities. The 93% is the manifestation of our sense of self. Yet, it is the part of our communication discussed the least, but others experience the most.

You see, your voice holds the truth of who you are. Your voice is the expression of how you respond in situations. It is the outward representation of your thoughts. It is the actualization of your intentions and the revelation of your behavior. Your voice is the indicator of your heart and the reflection of your spirit. You are a sum total of your voice and your voice is the personification of who and what you are. For these reasons, it is critically important for you to know how to effectively and strategically position your voice in a way that allows you to harness its power to master its influence.

Using vs. *Positioning*

I want to further clarify the difference between *using* your voice and *positioning* your voice. To *use* your voice means it can happen instinctively. *Use* of voice is not always connected to thoughtfulness or mindfulness. The use of voice can simply be a human function that is triggered by the brain in response to internal and/or external stimuli.

However, *positioning* your voice requires strategy, critical thought, and mindfulness. *Positioning* takes into consideration the situation, the place, the environment, and/or the person. *Positioning* does not mean simply gaining skill in speaking up, or speaking out, or speaking louder. *Positioning* is not simply about listening with an open posture and good eye-contact. Instead, *positioning* involves:

- Operating in your authenticity–Standing in your truth
- Being emotionally intelligent under pressure–Navigating your triggers
- Posturing for the end at the beginning–Determining your outcome
- Courageously confronting limitations–Conquering your fear
- Intentionally showing up as an asset and not a liability–Setting your tone
- Engaging your mind, body, and spirit–Listening to your whole self
- Giving yourself permission to shine–Controlling your own volume

Effectively *positioning* allows you to maximize every aspect of your voice by regenerating your 7%, transforming your 93% and freeing yourself to powerfully live your 100%.

The Voice Positioning System™
A framework for thoughtfully and mindfully situating your authentic voice for optimal impact and outcomes, The Voice Positioning System ™ is composed of seven actions:

1) Knowing your voice–*Voice Authenticity*
2) Trusting your voice–*Voice Confidence*
3) Creating space for your voice–*Voice Visibility*
4) Protecting your voice–*Voice Security*
5) Nurturing your voice–*Voice Management*
6) Celebrating your voice–*Voice Victories*
7) Amplifying the voices of others–*Voice Freedom*

Applied in a systematic and consistent way, these seven actions serve as a guide for positioning your authentic voice, as you harness your power and master your influence. While these actions are a framework, it is imperative that you do the work. Reclaiming your authentic voice will require your commitment to deconstructing your old narrative and reconstructing your new voice story. This process is not an easy one. However, I believe you are up for the challenge. I believe this is the reason you picked up this book. Keep reading… your VOICE is about to change!

AUTHOR'S NOTE

In 2008, my first book, *This is for YOU! 31 Days of Life Changing Discoveries* was published. The intention for the book was that it would serve as a thought-provoking and inspirational resource for those who were ready for the next level on their life's journey. Over the years, *This is for YOU!* readers have shared with me how the book transformed their thinking, their actions, and their lives

Perhaps you are asking what that book has to do with this book. If you are, I am glad you asked! No, this is not a commercial for *This is for YOU!* (Although I would love for you to pick up a copy). I share this bit of history with you, so I can provide some context for the introduction of this book.

In the introduction of *This is for YOU!*, I share a pivotal story from my childhood. The story captured a crucial time in my development. Embedded in injustice and racism, the experience set in motion a trajectory that would serve to catalyze my *misunderstanding* of my voice.

For this reason, I thought it most appropriate to share this story again in the introduction of this book. I thought it most important to share it as my own voice story. Why? Because throughout the pages of this book, I will ask you to examine your voice stories and perhaps hearing my story will serve as an inspiration in the exploration of your own.

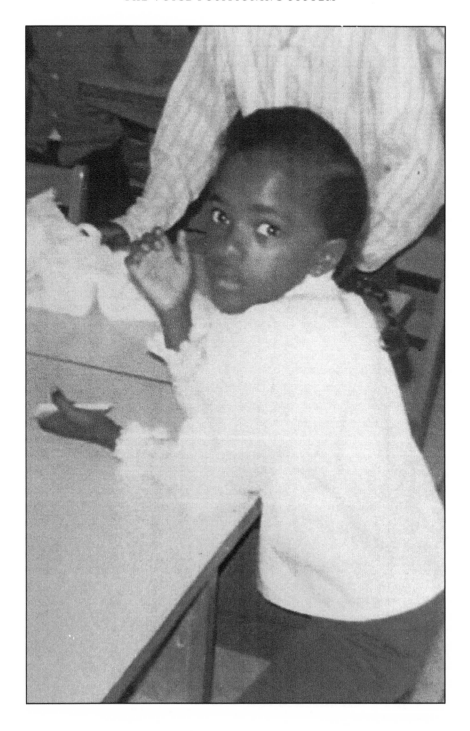

INTRODUCTION

On the third day of my first week of second grade, my mother scurried through the house in an effort to get me ready for school. We were both still trying to get used to the idea of my being dropped off at my grandma's house to catch the school bus. This was a different schedule than the one to which we had grown accustomed. Although we lived in a small rural town, prior to this time I had been able to ride into the city with my mother to go to school. On her way, she would drop me off at the door of my first-grade class.

My elementary school was a quality historically black school that was strategically placed in the middle of the inner city. It was a testament to the community and was just blocks away from my mother's office at one of the top historically black colleges in South Carolina.

As we walked to the car, my mother asked me a second time, "Are you sure you have everything you need?"

I said, "Yes, Ma'am," and we were on our way.

She pulled into the driveway at Grandma's house, helped me with the car door, kissed me goodbye, and began her commute.

Grandma greeted me at the door with a big smile and her usual, "Hurry in here so you can eat before that bus gets here." Grandma was also responsible for putting two of my cousins on the bus as well. So, we all sat and ate together with Grandma hurrying us along every thirty seconds. We giggled at her threats of not taking us to school if we missed the bus.

As we finished our breakfast, grabbed our books, and headed for the door, it hit me—I didn't have anything for the first day of show and tell. Immediately, I reflected on my mom's deliberate reminder earlier and began to cry. It was my intent to hide my tears from Grandma, but absolutely nothing ever got past her.

She quickly asked, "Child, what's wrong with you?"

I explained to her that I had left my item for show and tell at home.

"Is that all?"

She quickly looked around the room with her hands perched on her hips. Because all the community kids played here, and because she threw absolutely nothing away that came into her possession, I'm sure she believed she could find me something in a hurry. She walked over to the corner where my male cousins had been playing and picked up an item and put it in my hand. "Here, take this to show and tell—now come on so you can catch that bus."

When I looked in my hand, I saw that Grandma had handed me the largest marble I had ever seen. It was utterly beautiful. It was blue, black, and grey. Although I didn't exactly know what I was going to tell about it, I knew that I couldn't wait for everybody in my class to see it.

As the bus pulled up to the breezeway in the back of the school, I got the same nervous, sinking feeling that I had felt two days before. Things just weren't the same since my parents had been required to enroll me in this elementary school. It was zoned for integration. This school had been occupied by white people only. However, almost a year after Dr. Martin Luther King Jr.'s death, here we were.

I walked into my class, put my marble and books in the cubby portion of my desk, and took my seat. We began the day with the Lord's Prayer, the Pledge of Allegiance, and the singing of My Country 'Tis of Thee.

My teacher was a tall, older Caucasian woman with shiny silver hair. She probably would have appeared more attractive to me had it not been for the seemingly constant scowl on her face. She did not try to hide her disdain toward those of us who were new to the school. Nevertheless, I believed this day would be different. I would be able to stand in front of the class and talk, show my marble, win my teacher's affection, and make new friends in the process.

At the end of the scholastic portion of the day, finally it was time for show and tell. The teacher announced that we could take out our items and wait our turn to be called upon. She began to give us directives regarding the order we would come to the front. However, as she was completing her instructions, the white boy sitting next to me reached over into my desk's cubby and took my marble. After a few seconds of disbelief, I emphatically stated, "That is my marble. You can't have my marble." While staking my claim, I raised my hand to get the teacher's attention.

After a moment, she acknowledged my hand by asking, "What is it?" I told her that my classmate had just taken my marble out of my desk. She walked over to where we were both sitting and asked him if he had taken my marble. His words to her were an emphatic, "No, I did not take that nigger's marble."

She turned to me and sternly uttered, "Don't you ever lie to me again." She turned and walked away.

I watched silently as this little boy told a story and showed the class my marble. I was absolutely devastated. In my six years on earth, I had never felt that kind of pain. In a matter of moments, my entire world had been re-framed. I had been robbed of my innocence, security, and stability and left with guilt, fear, and uncertainty. The heated rod of injustice had branded the core of my soul—into my will, my mind, and my emotions. As a result, I suffered the greatest loss of all... my *authentic* voice.

This lesson I learned about my voice set in motion a traumatic, arduous journey filled with a lack of power, confidence, purpose, independence, and peace. It veiled my eyes, ears, heart, and mind concerning the good plans that had been ordained for my life. I spent a significant amount of time in search of reassurance. I searched for self-assurance. I searched for direction. I searched for autonomy. I searched for authenticity. I searched for permanence. I searched and searched for the same beauty and awe in life I saw in my marble that day in 1969. I searched with a drive and determination to get my marble back.

The Story Doesn't End There

For decades, the impact of my lost marble showed up in my life. Whether in my personal or professional life, the absence of my authentic voice showed up in every space in which I found myself–home, family, work, and church–every space. Not that I was tucked away in a corner with an inability to speak. I was still showing up. But, I was showing up with diminished value while my authentic voice remained unheard and invisible.

My inauthentic voice compromised my physical, emotional, and mental health, while I lived in my own secret asylum, allowing my authentic voice to be mishandled and mismanaged. Not positioning my voice according to my original design dimmed the light inside of me. I learned to speak through other people's voices because I believed they had a sound better than my own. I wore a mask with other people's faces on it because how they showed up seemed to be more powerful than my presence. I hid the beautiful gift of my authentic voice because I was traumatized into believing it was not good enough.

Quiet Takeover

Consider this… In 1955, Jack Finney published the classic science fiction novel, *Invasion of the Body Snatchers*. The plot is centered on alien life-forms who quietly take over the bodies and minds of humans while they are sleeping. In the takeover process, the human is left devoid of all human emotion. The takeover is not realized immediately; it is only noticeable when the human ceases to exhibit the characteristics they once did.

My question for you is, have you been sleeping while your voice has been snatched? Allow me to help you assess whether you have had your own invasion. Consider these indicators:

1. When you are unable to muster up the courage to say "no" to a person when everything in you is screaming, yet you silence the noise of your own opposition with your usual, "yes".

2. When you trade the truth in exchange for telling lies because it is what another person wants to hear, and you don't want to risk displeasing them and losing the relationship.
3. When you respond swiftly to the beck and call of someone else while neglecting your own sense of well-being.
4. When your own needs become secondary because you have allowed others to convince you that their needs are more important.
5. When you diminish your God-given gifts, talents, and abilities because you have allowed others to convince you to dull your shine.
6. When you find yourself giving far more than what you are receiving in return.
7. When you walk away from your own potential to grow and reach your goals, simply because you have surrounded yourself with people who have no desire to pursue their own.
8. When you feel trapped inside yourself because your missing voice has rendered you emotionally disabled with an inability to escape.

If you found yourself in any or all of these areas, can you see how your authentic voice has been snatched?

The deep pain of living a life God never created me to live became the catalyst for me to reclaim my sound—my authentic voice. Now, I will not mislead you into thinking the journey was an easy one. It was a process and required my commitment to doing the work. I had to begin with telling myself the truth—the truth that I was not living an authentic life—my best life. My message to the world was not real and the greater truth is, I was tired from the weight of the mask.

It was not until I came face-to-face with the reality that not being authentic was killing me that I knew I had to make a change. My mind, my will, and my emotions were suffering in silence. The energy it took to wear the mask had taken its toll on my spirit. I was not living in my power and I had little positive influence in the life of others. Most of all, I was tired of living a life that contradicted my truth.

So, my pursuit was to reclaim what had been snatched from me, to harness my personal power, and to position my authentic voice in a way that would positively influence the lives of those around me and those on the paths I had yet to cross. So, the truth of the matter is, I wake up every day with great intention to accomplish the following 7 things:

1) Know my voice
2) Trust my voice
3) Create space for my voice
4) Protect my voice
5) Nurture my voice
6) Celebrate my voice
7) Amplify the voice of others.

Why? Because my Authentic Voice Freedom depends on it!

Reclaiming Your Voice

What is your authentic voice worth to you? Is it worth the sacrifices you will have to make? Is it worth the risks you will have to take? Well, if you are ready and willing to commit to doing the work, you will need these three things:

1. **A Fearless Heart** - This is where you embrace your value to the degree that you become relentlessly unwavering in standing your ground while facing any person, place, or thing that would attempt to rob you of your authenticity. You push back every deeply entrenched notion that you are not enough and that you are inadequate. This does not mean that you have no fear. It simply means that the more you step into your courage, you *fear less*. This is the place where you fully show up to RECLAIM your authentic voice!

2. **A Future Story** - This is where you recognize that your future story can be far greater than the narrative others have attempted to lock you into. It is here that you take the pen out of anyone's hand who is not co-authoring your happily ever-after. This is the

place where you write new chapters as you RECLAIM your authentic voice!

3. **A Freedom Mindset** – This is where you free yourself to *be* yourself. You take off the shackles that have held your mind captive to a history that has consistently served to sabotage your success. Here is where you commit to walk in the truth of who God created you to be and to do it unapologetically, RECLAIMING your authentic voice!

You must be vigilant in your pursuit to reclaim your authentic voice in order to position it in a way that allows you to harness your power and master your influence. I am not willing to give up what rightfully belongs to me. Are you? I am certain your answer is, "NO!" Okay then… Let's go! I am going to be right here with you as you take this journey to reclaiming your authentic voice, harnessing your power, and mastering your influence.

CHAPTER ONE

*Knowing Your Voice
(Voice Authenticity)*

CHAPTER ONE
Knowing Your Voice (Voice Authenticity)

You have the power to write a new chapter in your voice story. ~Dr. K

Let's get right to it! Now that you've read the introduction of this book, take a moment and respond to these questions. What is your "marble" story? As you think back, several stories may come to your mind. On the other hand, you may not be able to think of any stories at all. If this is the case, let's go a little deeper and I'll ask a different way. *When was the first time someone or something broke your voice?*

When I refer to a broken voice, I am referring to a fracture of any aspect of your mind, your will, or your emotions? I am referring to trauma to your soul that came in the form of negative messages passed down to you, words from others that shattered your spirit, or hurt from a relationship that rocked your world. I am referring to the damage done to your confidence as a result of being devalued, ignored, or treated as if you were invisible. I am referring to the fragmentation of your peace, your joy, and your sense of well-being. The truth is, we all have a human need to be seen and heard. When we are not, something inside us breaks. So, I ask, "Who or what broke your voice?"

Even as I'm asking you these questions, I feel my own stories and the well of emotions that come with them. I still remember. In truth, I don't believe I will ever forget them. I won't forget because these stories remind me of the interruption of something. These stories remind me of an introduction to something. They remind me of a withdrawal from something. I remember them all. As we begin our journey together, I am inviting you to remember your own.

VOICE ACTION: At this moment, block out any noise around you. Go inside yourself. Yes, I understand that "inside yourself" may not be a place you visit often. That is exactly why I am asking you to go there now. With your eyes closed, engage your mind; engage your heart; engage your spirit; and ask yourself this question, *"What happened to my voice?"* Be still. Listen to your inner voice. Give it permission to tell you the truth. *What did you hear?* Write it down. This is the beginning of reclaiming what you lost.

_____

_____

_____

_____

_____

_____

_____

_____

Date:_____

Your Story Matters

We began with your voice story because telling yourself the truth about your voice is critical to your voice journey. I recognize your story may not be like my "marble" story or even remotely related to my story. But, I wanted to invite you to reflect over your life and to consider your own metaphorical stolen or lost "marbles" and how your experiences ultimately changed your voice.

I can imagine you may think I am assuming your voice may have changed over time. Well, I feel safe in making this assumption based upon the fact that you have read up to this point in the book. I am choosing to believe there is something that has intrigued you about this notion of reclaiming your authentic voice and harnessing your power so you can master your influence. If I am correct, then this means somewhere along the way something happened that impacted your authentic voice.

I am aware your reflection and discovery may feel heavy. I want to assure you this book is not going to be filled with doom and gloom. But, it is important that we go back for a moment before we move forward. While I am not an advocate of living in the past, I do believe there are times when it is necessary to revisit the past so we can extract the valuable lessons that are always present in our past experiences. Those times of trauma, shame, guilt, abuse, rejection, pain, and humiliation that are a tragic part of our yesterday have within them lessons that contain the power to strengthen us when we face challenges in our today.

Digging through the rubble of our "once upon a time" often facilitates our understanding of where it all went wrong, but most importantly, where it all began. So, as we embark upon our journey together through the pages of this book, I believe it is needful for us to go back to the beginning – all the way back to where it all started.

You Were Not Born This Way

We were not born with broken voices. In fact, one of the ways newborn babies are assessed for good health is their robust cry (voice). If a newborn does not cry or does not cry robustly within the first thirty seconds to one minute of life, it is a cause for alarm.

This means that when we showed up in the world, we came with a sound – our very own sound – one that was unique to us. This sound was so special; it could immediately grab the attention of those around us. When others heard it, they stopped to attend to us. The sound was so distinct; mothers could recognize it amongst the many sounds of other babies in the same room. We were identified with that sound. Although we were born with powerful voice identity, somewhere along the way, someone and/or something convinced us we needed to change our unique and authentic sound. The tragedy is, we believed what we heard, and we did what they said.

Voice Lessons

We may have heard messages like, "Children should be seen and not heard." We may have been told, "Children should stay in their place." Or, we may have learned, "It's disrespectful to talk back", or that we should "only speak when we are spoken to." We may have even been taught, "Big boys and girls don't cry." As a result, we were expected to adjust our sound. We were expected to change its uniqueness and its beauty. We were expected to turn our sound down, to mute it, or turn it off.

You see, I distinctly remember being a happy-go-lucky little girl. I was carefree and isolated from the ills of our society in the 1960s. I was oblivious to the power of words to break something inside. In my "country-girl" upbringing, surrounded by my family and a village who watched over me, words made me feel safe; they made me feel loved. So, it wasn't until I felt the sting of a word that day in the second grade that I experienced its power to shatter my voice and to take pieces of it away.

I didn't realize the power of one word to silence me. I did not realize the power of a word to shift my identity. But, here is the thing – as much as that single word hurt, the deeper wound was related to my teacher not believing my truth. Her actions not only broke my heart, they broke my voice.

Broken Voices, Break Us!

When my voice broke that day in second grade, it was also the day my internal conversations changed. As a result, my sound changed. My authenticity disappeared. My broken voice led me to create a new narrative:

- "It's bad to be me."
- "If being a Black girl is a bad thing, then I want to be a White girl."
- "If I become who others want me to be, they'll like me."

I took these pieces from my broken voice and used them to rewrite my story. This new story took the place of everything I once believed about myself. The detriment of this new narrative was that it muted my authentic voice while simultaneously turning up the volume on a voice I had allowed my circumstances to create. My lessons from my broken voice had taught me to wear a mask. And, you know what? Our authentic voice will never sound the same when a mask is covering it.

Voice Action: We were all born with our own unique sound. Our sound was a representation of our presence and place in the world. At some point, we learned lessons about our sound – our authentic voice. Reflect for a moment, *what were the very first lessons you learned about your voice?* Think very deeply here. At what point and in what ways *did those lessons cause you to change your sound?* Now, consider this - *How are those lessons showing up in your life today?* Write it down. If these are the lessons that caused you to change your sound and mask your voice, these will also be the lessons you will have to "unlearn" in order to reclaim your sound – your authentic voice.

_____

_____

_____

_____

_____

_____

Counterfeit Voice

A façade, a front, a masquerade, a fake – that is what masking my voice identity produced in me. Of course, these were not the "public" words I used to describe myself. This was certainly not the way I introduced myself to others. Yet, these were the "ugly" words – the ones I chose to keep hidden and the ones I desperately guarded, hoping they were never uncovered for fear of being exposed.

You see, these were the silent words. The ones left unspoken. These were the words that rose to the surface of my thinking and settled in my gut each time I flashed the huge inauthentic smile across my face in the middle of telling someone how "okay" or how "fine" I was. These hushed words showed up in the mirror when I looked at myself. I saw with my eyes a self- manufactured picture of perfection – every hair in place, flawlessly beautiful makeup, and outfits that were super- model-ready. But, on the other hand, there was another face looking back at me, a person covered in an unseen garment of heaviness, the weight of which existed just below the surface of what was seen in my reflection.

These words were the ones I would dare not bring to the light because I would run the risk of letting others in on my well-kept secret – I was really not who you they thought I was. Consequently, I used my energy guarding the secret with my life, or rather in spite of my life. I became a player of the game and a master of disguise – while drowning in the same water I had allowed others to believe I walked on. I had convinced myself that the high price I paid for my external performance at the expense of my authentic voice identity was worth it.

Performance-Driven

When we give up our authentic voice, we become performers in our own drama. We perform for those who love us. We perform for those who hate us. We perform for those who are completely indifferent toward us. Encore after encore, we return to the stage for these audiences, drooling over their applause, longing for their acceptance, or to capture their attention. We curtsy and bow in response to the temporary high of adulation. We look frantically for the "thumbs up" from our harshest critics. We linger on stage only to find that when the scene ends, and the curtain closes, and the crowd goes away, like a costume, we lay down the mask and come face-to-face with ourselves.

Who is that person? Where does she belong? Where is her place in this world? Where does she fit? What is her purpose? What has she been sent to this world to accomplish? What is her value? What is her worth? Where is her authentic voice? These are the questions that bombard our minds. But before we can stop long enough to give a response, we hear the crowd gathering again for another show. And, because we have grown accustomed to only brief intermissions of sincere contemplation about the power of our voice, we rise with vigor for the next act – Lights, Camera, Action – We're on!

Separating ourselves from ourselves, we trade our real voice identity for the allure of the crowd, never even recognizing the tragedy of our counterfeit voice. Furthermore, this insistent need to please slowly becomes a deadly disease to please a subtle destroyer of our authentic voice. You become oppressed. This oppression will rob you of your fight because it robs you of your power.

Your REAL Voice

The journey to authenticity and answering the questions life poses requires our brutal honesty. It requires work. We cannot expect to get to an authentic response if we are unwilling to confront the fraudulent voices we are allowing to define our identity.

While many of us fear confrontation or try to avoid it at all costs, reclaiming your voice is worth the encounter. It is worth confronting yourself. Your *real* voice has been covered long enough. Your *real* voice has lingered in the background while you have put on "the other you" like Cover Girl makeup – while knowing deep down within, it is not all "Easy...Breezy... Beautiful." Your *real* voice longs to break through. Your *real* voice longs to be free.

Voice Action: Are you ready? Take a moment here and think about the ways you have protected a voice that is not even your own. Now, step into your courage to tell yourself the truth about the following: *In what ways have you covered your authentic voice?*

_____

_____

_____

_____

_____

Whatever your responses were to this question, I hope you were able to see ways in which your authentic voice has been suffering. I hope you were able to see how you have been contributing to your own voice crisis. Most importantly, I hope you identified within yourself, a sincere desire to reconnect your life to your authentic voice. I hope you recognized the urgency to reclaim it.

Voice Positioning Points for
CONVERSATIONS WITH YOURSELF

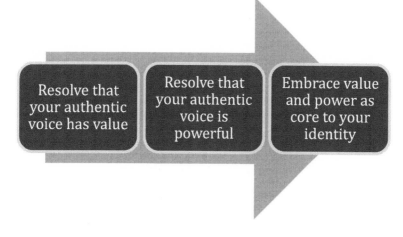

| Resolve that your authentic voice has value | Resolve that your authentic voice is powerful | Embrace value and power as core to your identity |

Voice Positioning Point One: Resolve That Your Authentic Voice Has Value

Today, and for the rest of your days, you will need to wake up with the resolution that your authentic voice is priceless. This will serve as a daily affirmation that your presence has meaning. It is an ongoing acknowledgment that you embody something no one else in the world has. You are the holder of a unique design and the carrier of a Divine masterpiece. It is your most prized possession. It is the keeper of the light that is meant to shine in darkness. It is the radiance that changes the atmosphere when you walk into a room. It's time to resolve that your authentic voice has value!

Voice Positioning Point Two: Resolve That Your Authentic Voice is Powerful

If you are serious about positioning your voice in a way that allows you to harness your power and master your influence, you must resolve once-and-for-all that your voice is powerful. You must know your power is not arrogant, conceited, or boastful. It only becomes those things when it is misused and misaligned. Instead, your authentic voice is powerful in truth, purity, and beauty. Its genuineness is your hallmark and the certainty of it is the authoritative force that enables you to speak life and allow your life to speak. It's time to resolve that your authentic voice is powerful!

Voice Positioning Point Three: Embrace Value and Power as Core to Your Identity

Willingly and enthusiastically hold your authentic voice *value* and *power* as the central and most important attributes of your identity. Establish an intention to lead your life with this truth. Commit to not allowing anyone or anything to diminish, disregard, or debase these undeniable gifts that are yours. It is your responsibility to hold on to them.

It's time to embrace value and power as core to your identity!

When Silence Kills

When we remain silent, while knowing the truth, our silence keeps us hidden. It is our unwillingness to speak that keeps our authentic voice barricaded inside ourselves. It is our stifled voice of truth that causes us to linger in a state of secrecy while completely disregarding the fact that silence kills. When we are silent about our truth, we make room for other things inside us to die. Our courage dies, our confidence dies, and our genuineness dies. Remaining silent robs us of joy and freedom. Being silent sabotages the "good success" we were intended to have.

Silence weakens us and sucks the life out of us. Being silent paralyzes us and keeps us mired deeply in our dysfunction. Silence gives others permission to control us, manipulate us, use us, and abuse us. This silence is not golden. There is nothing about it that resembles beauty. In the end, it only serves to leave us void of power and keeps us fearful, covered, and in hiding.

In fact, many of the "voice lessons" we have learned over the course of our life have robbed us of the precious gift of knowing our voice, our identity, and the very essence of who we are. These lessons have interjected doubt and tampered with our confidence. We have questioned the value and worth of our voice. We have minimized it when maximizing it really mattered. We have suppressed it and even hidden it because we did not believe in it.

We have surrendered it to the "power of they" – What will they say? What will they do? How will they feel? What will they think? But, in surrendering to "they", we create our own internal struggle; a struggle that keeps the light of our voice muted. Not knowing our voice renders us helpless and hopeless. It depletes our energy and causes us to become complacent as we acquiesce to the weight of our own silence.

From the Research
I had the privilege of conducting a research study with amazing women who shared their stories of suffering in silence at work. They candidly spoke of feeling fragmented and unable to bring all of who they were to the workplace. Many of them found themselves not fully engaging their brilliance. They were denying themselves the power of fully showing up. They felt as though their light was dimmed and the fire inside them was extinguished. They disclosed how their silence interfered with their sense of value and confidence. Their silence was the manifestation of their broken voices.

The Caged Bird

In her autobiographical work, "I Know Why the Caged Bird Sings" – Dr. Maya Angelou explained her reasons for ceasing to speak, "The only thing I could do was stop talking…If I talked to anyone else, that person might die. Just my breath, carrying my words out, might poison people and they'd curl up and die."

This feeling of being caged in silence was very real to me. For decades, my voice lived behind metaphorical bars; locked down with fear, in a place I believed I was powerless to leave. As the "caged bird", the lyrics of my songs were filled with the loss of confidence, self-doubt, and self-minimizing. Like a broken record, all of my tunes played to the rhythm of internalized pain. I was stuck. I was unable to be free. That is, until I finally recognized I had the key.

You've Got the Key!

I often ask my clients this critical question, "Where is your key?" In other words, where have you placed your personal power? Where have you placed that intrinsic force inside of you that makes the whole of who you are? Where did you leave your voice? Where did you lose your identity?

Several years ago, I was on my way to my office when I received a call with a frantic voice on the other end: "Mom, I can't find my house key." Immediately, I began asking questions to assist my daughter in back-tracking her steps to determine where her key could have been misplaced. With every question I asked came the response, "I looked there already." At the end of this exhaustive process, I told her that she would just have to wait until I could get there to pick her up. I told her I loved her and ended the call.

But, after really thinking about the situation, I came to the realization that her lost key had set in motion a set of circumstances that had changed the course of the day for us both. Because of a lost key, she had been denied access to a place in which she was previously entitled to enter. The security of our home was now at risk because of the possibility that the key could have fallen into the wrong hands.

This metaphorical key represents the power you have to unlock those areas in your life that have held your voice captive. But, far too many of us have lost our keys and they have possibly fallen into the wrong hands. So, the question I want to ask you, "Where is your key?" Answering this question opens the way to the most critical conversation you can ever have – the one you have with yourself.

Voice Positioning Points for
CONVERSATIONS WITH YOURSELF

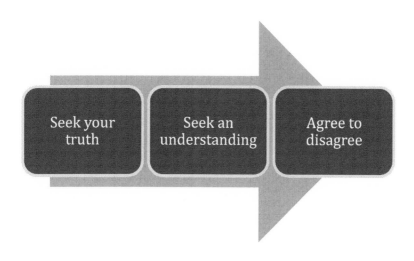

| Seek your truth | Seek an understanding | Agree to disagree |

Voice Positioning Point One: Seek Your Truth

Every critical conversation you will ever have with yourself has to begin by seeking to know your truth. While this sounds like an easy task on the surface, the truth of the matter is sometimes our truth is very hard to find. This is because we are not always honest with ourselves, or we make excuses for the things we know, making the truth null and void. Because we don't want to feel the discomfort the truth often brings, we keep it at a distance and we work around it. Perhaps we believe if we wait long enough, it will just go away. But here is the thing. I can assure you that you are better off seeking your truth than your truth showing up when you least expect it. At least when you seek truth, you can use what you know for your benefit and sense of well-being. When truth finds you, it often brings exposure. It's time to seek your truth.

Voice Positioning Point Two: Seek an Understanding

Once you have discovered your truth, seek to understand what it means for your life. What is your life speaking to you? What are you speaking back to your life? It is here where you ask yourself critical questions and you respond to yourself with your most transparent answers. It is here where you listen. It is here where you assess your feelings. It is here where you make every effort to sort through and understand your "why." In other words, why you do what you do, why you are the way you are, and why you need to position your voice for impact. You will lose your way if you lose your why. It's time to seek an understanding.

Voice Positioning Point Three: Agree to Disagree

When you have gained an understanding, you must agree with yourself that you will be intentional in disagreeing with anything that is contrary to your truth. This is the dialogue you have with yourself when you face situations that threaten what you know to be true about who you are, your purpose, and your destiny. You commit to disagree with anything that comes your way that is misaligned with your path to freedom. It is here where you defend yourself against yourself. This is the place for powerful truth-telling by interrogating your own false inner critic. This is where you resist your own temptation to sabotage your voice freedom. In fact, this is the place where you fight for your freedom, recognizing the fight is really within yourself.

Unlock Your Voice Story

In a session with one of my coaching clients, we discovered that she was framing her life and decisions around an image she had of her father. Because he was not present for a portion of her childhood and beyond, she was navigating through her life governed by a fear of being like her father. As a result, she was living in a narrative that did not belong to her. She was living out of his story and not her own. In fact, she had lost sight of her own story.

I am a firm believer that we are the sum total of all our experiences. We are a conglomeration of each integral part of our past, every orchestration of our present, and all the potential and hope for our future – we are all of those things – housed in one wonderfully created dwelling place. However, life brings with it many opportunities for us to *not* know, or for us to forget, or for us to struggle with, or for us to ignore, or for us to not fully understand our own story and voice authenticity. However, when we unlock our voice story, we are able to delve deeply into those places of *"unspokeness"*, where screams from our souls emerge, but are rarely released out loud.

Our story houses our *Voice DNA,* the intricate details of our voice identity that are unique to us. Our story is comprised of our imaginary and real events. Our story is a multi-faceted narrative of fiction and non-fiction, heroes and villains; and nightmares and dreams. Our story is complex and layered. It is mired in defeat and embellished in victory. Nevertheless, with all our voice story holds for us, it will never fully unfold, until we step into the boldness to unlock it.

Voice Positioning Points for
CONVERSATIONS WITH YOURSELF

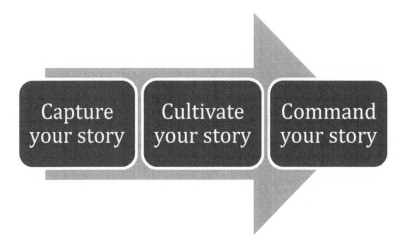

Voice Positioning Point One: Capture Your Story

Far too often, we live our lives inside the stories of others. Like characters created by the author, we become a part of a storyline with no voice in how the story will progress or end. Because we have been so ingrained in their narrative, we begin to believe their story is our own. Therefore, we forfeit our power to be the author of our own happily-ever-after. But, the truth of the matter is, their story is not ours. It is simply that our story remains untold. Yet, central to your authentic voice journey is the critical need to capture your story. It is time for you to take control of your narrative. It's time to unlock your story. The end.

Voice Positioning Point Two: Cultivate Your Story

Your story is a treasure chest of gifts for your journey. Inside our past chapters are invaluable lessons and blessings that serve as guides for writing and navigating the chapters that are to come. It is time for you to embrace your treasure. There are pieces that are tarnished and damaged. There are parts you have avoided and never verbalized out loud. There are entire chapters you wish you could delete. However, it's time to cultivate your story. It's time to take what has been in your life and build upon it with the power you have to rewrite what you want it to be. It's time to release your story and the guilt, shame, secrecy, or any aspect of it that has held you hostage. It's time to take the parts you can use and cultivate it to create a testimony that will speak life to others. It's time to unlock your story. The end.

Voice Positioning Point Three: Command Your Story

Take command of your story. No one can tell it like you can. Your lived experiences are priceless. You are the authority on your history and the author for your future. Take the pen out of anyone's hand who would attempt to write on the pages of your life without permission from you. Every day you wake up you are given a brand-new page. It is your responsibility to maximize that page. Be intentional with what you write on them. Stand in your authority to determine what you will include and what you will not. The choice is yours. It's time to unlock your story. The end.

From the Research

As a result of my research study, I learned that many of these stories began as subtle messages heard over time. Expressed through their individual journeys, women who participated in the study revealed the generational, historical, and cultural messages they learned about their voice. One study participant shared how she grew up living by the adage, "Children should be seen and not heard." She shared, "I don't really feel like I had a voice as a kid. We lived in a house where you just did what your parents told you to do." Similarly, another participant shared, "Growing up, I felt like my voice didn't matter, so I stopped using my voice. I just didn't think my voice was important. So, I really don't know what my voice sounds like."

Sound Control

I received a powerful revelation one day as I walked in my office. I leaned down and turned on the lamp sitting on the coffee table and I heard a humming sound coming from the light bulb. I clicked it off again to see if the same thing would happen. When I turned on the light again, the humming sound started. Immediately, the thought came to me that light has a sound. Each time the light was turned on, there was a sound associated with it. I could see light. But, I could also hear a sound.

Your voice, in its most authentic form, is intended to be light. Your voice carries the brilliance of the light of who we were created to be. The light of your voice is the instrument that has been given to you to illuminate darkness. Your voice has a sound even when you are not using words. The sound is powerful, but it is also detrimental to you when you don't know how to position it. Why? Because if we don't know, we become vulnerable to people, places, and things that will impose on us what they believe its position should be.

From the Research

While responding to interview questions from the research study, participants began to raise their own questions. One participant contemplated: "Have I lost my voice? Have I decided to conform? Have I changed myself? This is a scary place. There are times when I just silence myself from everybody and I didn't do that in the beginning. But now, I find myself at a place that has changed me."

My Hope For You...

At this very moment, I hope you're feeling a sense of urgency to know your voice – your authentic voice. I hope this chapter has started a fire in your belly. I hope you considered the areas of brokenness in your voice. I hope you've thought about the voice lessons of your past. I hope you removed your mask and diagnosed your disease to please others. I hope you considered your sound and your silence. Most importantly, I hope you are committed to knowing your voice. I hope you are recognizing the value of its authenticity.

TAKE YOUR POSITION!

Now it is time to do the work! Knowing your voice must be your first priority. Before you proceed to the next section of the book, you must take your position:

1. **Reclaim Your Authentic Voice** – The journey to knowing your authentic voice requires courage. Authentic voice shows up when you are truthful with yourself and truthful with others. The greatest deterrent to your authentic voice is fear. However, the first step in positioning your authentic voice with power and influence is to not let fear keep you from conquering those areas that have kept you from fully showing up in your most authentic way. Let the *truth* that your voice was created to be powerful, counteract the negative whispers that it is not. Even if the fear remains for a moment, keep affirming your authentic truth until your fear disappears. Know this, fear cannot remain when you allow your power to override it. You've got this!

2. **Harness Your Power** – No matter how much you get to know about your authentic voice, you harness your power by giving yourself permission to stand in your *truth*. In order to stand, you will need to take back your power from people, places, and/or things. Taking your power back may also mean losing some people, places, and things in the process. Whatever the case, know this, nothing is worth holding on to if it compromises your voice authenticity. You've got this!

3. **Master Your Influence** – You have the power to positively influence others through intentionally and thoughtfully positioning your voice. Although your voice authenticity may cost you something, know this, people are attracted to what is real. You've got this!

MY VOICE COMMITMENT LETTER

Dear _____

Today, I commit to:

_____

_____

_____

_____

_____

_____

_____

_____

_____

_____

Love,

_____

CHAPTER TWO

Trusting Your Voice (Voice Confidence)

CHAPTER TWO
Trusting Your Voice (Voice Confidence)

Trusting your voice begins with changing your mind. ~Dr. K

Your life has a voice. Your life is always speaking to you. All around you, in every turn, with each step, you will find your life's voice. You can hear it in everything you do. Your life speaks and echoes from every decision and choice you make. Your life speaks through your conversations, through every word you utter, and through every word you keep to yourself. Your life speaks through the ways in which you think. Your life speaks in your behavior and your actions. Most importantly, and of greatest relevancy to this book, is the fact that your life is speaking each time you make the choice not to trust your authentic voice.

When your life speaks, it is the measure by which you can readily determine if you are living a life of truth or if you are living a life of consequences. When your life speaks to you, its voice is loaded with information you need for self-assessment, for discernment, for reflection, for correction, and for change. When your life speaks to you, its messages carry everything you need in your pursuit of authenticity. The challenge is in learning to trust what you hear.

Who or What to Trust

I was invited as a guest speaker for a women's conference for a thriving ministry in Augusta, GA. This ministry has a cutting-edge message for people who are seeking to live a Christian life in today's world. The theme for this annual women's conference, "Perfecting MySpace," was symbolic of this distinction.

During a conversation with the pastor's wife, she shared with me that the theme emerged out of her desire to address the craze around the world's use of technology and social media. In the midst of creating profiles that revealed information (fact or fiction) about who they were, she wanted women to come together to examine and explore their own inner spaces—mind, will, and emotions. As such, she chose three speakers to elaborate on each of those areas – mind, will, and emotions. My topic was, "Perfecting My Mind."

As the first speaker, I began the presentation by telling the audience that it was not my intention to insult their intelligence; but because I am a teacher at heart, I wanted to begin by giving them a definition of the mind. I shared with them that the mind is defined as, "The seat of consciousness in which thinking and feeling takes place." I explained that as women, we are known for being thinkers and feelers. We are quick to say things such as, "This is what I think." "This is how I feel." "I think you should..." "I feel like you ought to..." But, if the mind is the *seat* of consciousness where thinking and feeling takes place, then my question to you is "who or what is sitting on your seat?" In other words, who or what is really on your mind? The conference was awesome, and I believe I left the women with much to ponder and implement. But, there are take-aways from what I shared with that audience that I want you to consider.

The brain is the most complex part of the human body. This three-pound organ houses intelligence, is the interpreter of the senses, is the initiator of body movement, and is the controller of behavior. Lying in its bony shell and washed by protective fluid, the brain is the source of all qualities that define our humanity. It is actually the crown jewel of our anatomy. So then, our brains house our mentality, intuition, perception, conception, capacity, judgment, understanding, wisdom, reasoning, wit, creativity, ingenuity, and memory. Yet, in the midst of all these things going on in our heads, we have some other things on our minds—sitting in the seats of our consciousness.

If you are wondering what the brain has to do with your voice, I am happy to tell you – everything. You see, since the brain is the seat of consciousness where thinking and feeling takes place, then you have to assess who or what you have allowed to sit in that seat and to occupy space in your head, especially if that occupant is muting your authentic voice and minimizing your confidence.

Who? Or What?

Let's delve deeper. When you consider "Who?" – Ask yourself these questions:

1. Who am I afraid to share my authentic voice with?
2. Who has the most influence on how I respond when I have a seat at a table?
3. Who is on my mind when I am making the decision about how I am going to show-up in a room?
4. Who am I mimicking?
5. Who am I dumbing-down for?
6. Who am I shrinking back from?
7. Who has made me feel invisible?
8. Who said I was not enough?

Answering these "Who" questions is critical because your voice confidence is attached to your responses. Whoever you identify as your answer, is also the same "Who" occupying space in your head and robbing you of your personal power. Even greater than that is the fact that when your "Who" sits in your head, it sits on your authentic voice. Knowing this might also explain why you've felt like you have so much to say…and an inability to get it out.

Consider the following intruders that are notorious for invading our space:

- Hurt from past relationships
- Physical, mental, psychological, and emotional abuse
- Unresolved family issues
- Current relationships that are not conducive to our well-being

Voice Action: Who is your "Who"? It is time to identify the culprit sitting in your head. This assessment may take you a moment because you may have normalized the presence of your "Who" – However, I want to remind you that anything that sits on your authentic voice should not be welcomed in your space. Here is your chance to issue an eviction notice and take your space back! *Begin the process of writing your eviction notice(s) here:*

Dear _____,

_____

_____

_____

_____

_____

_____

Congratulations for identifying your "who"! However, you are not finished yet. Remember, there was also a "What?" – In other words, *what* messages have you allowed to bombard your brain and sabotage your confidence? When you consider "What" - ask yourself these questions:

1. What devaluing words have you allowed to deplete your spirit?
2. What negative behaviors of others have you accommodated and enabled?
3. What situations have you allowed that cause you great shame?
4. What has gotten in the way of your courage?
5. What has broken your heart?
6. What has caused you to lose sight of your power?

Proverbs 23:7 states, "As {she} thinks in {her} heart, so is {she}." In essence, we become whatever we think about. If you have allowed devaluing words, negative behaviors of others, shame, lack of courage, broken heart, or loss of vision to consume your thinking, then that is what your voice becomes. Let me further explain. Your "What" has a way of, whispering in your ear, things that are contrary to your authentic voice. However, the whispering is not the issue. The issue is when you believe "What" you hear. It is at this point that you give permission for that thought to take up residence in your head. This is where the struggle begins.

The moment we entertain those thoughts, we offer them a "Beverly Hillbillies" invitation - "Sit a spell. Take your shoes off" (okay, you may not remember this line from the show). The point is this; we allow those thoughts to occupy headspace. The greater issue is the longer these thoughts remain, they not only occupy headspace; they begin to occupy heart space, spirit space, soul space, and ultimately, authentic voice space.

We become comfortable with the presence of these thoughts and we don't recognize all the ways our "occupants" are changing our demeanor, disposition, attitude, and character. Furthermore, we protect their presence by telling ourselves and others "That's just the way I am." But the truth is, that is not the truth. It is just familiar, and we hold on to "What" is familiar and to "What" is comfortable. We hold on to our "What" even when holding on is destroying something inside of us.

In a *Voice Positioning Leadership Program* I was facilitating, I shared Harriett Tubman's rules for the journey when she was transporting slaves to freedom in the Underground Railroad. She made it perfectly clear that if they were going to embark upon the journey with her, they had to be committed. She ensured their commitment by showing them the gun she carried. She made certain they understood that if they started the journey with her and then decided they were going to turn around, she would kill them. That's how committed she was to freedom.

I feel like the "Harriet Tubman of Voice." No, I am not threatening your life. I simply want you to be so committed to your own freedom that turning back at this point would feel like death to you. I want you to want it. I want you to pursue it like your life depends on it. I want you to feel the heavy bondage of having your voice enslaved to an owner who is not you. I want you to go after your freedom.

This journey begins with *what* you're thinking. Philippians 4:8 states, "Whatever things are true, whatever things are noble, whatever things are just, whatever things are pure, whatever things are lovely, whatever things are of good report, if there is any virtue and if there is anything praiseworthy—think on these things."

Whatever your "What" is, it is time to confront it. If you allow it to continue to occupy your space, your life will continue to go in the direction of that choice. If you continue to make excuses for "What" is occupying your space, your life will continue to go in the direction of that choice. If you continue to believe as you have always believed about "What" is occupying your space, your life will continue to go in the direction of that choice. If you want different results, you must get rid of "What" is sitting in your way.

Voice Action: What is your "What"? It is time to identify the culprit sitting in your head. This assessment may take you a moment because you may have normalized the presence of your "What" – However, I want to remind you that anything that sits on your authentic voice should not be welcomed in your space. Here is your chance to issue an eviction notice and take your space back! *Begin the process of writing your eviction notice(s) here:*

Dear _____,

_____

_____

_____

_____

_____

What To Do With Fear

At the center of your "who' and "what" is the elephant that does not always get named – FEAR. We very seldom acknowledge the power fear has in our lives. In fact, we tend to cover it well. But, think about how hard it is to hide an elephant.

When I was a little girl, I loved listening to fairytales and nursery rhymes. One of my favorite stories was "The Three Little Pigs." Because it came in audio form, I could play the album on the stereo, read the accompanying book, look at the illustrations, and sing along with the music. I thought the pigs were adorable, and I loved the houses they built out of sticks, straw, and bricks. But I also remember the horror I felt every time the Big Bad Wolf entered the scene. At that time, the music would change from happy to daunting. The pictures would show the wolf creeping up on the houses in which the pigs felt secure. Because they were not alert, they didn't even know he was outside. Although I always knew how the story was going to end, I was still afraid every time the Big Bad Wolf threatened to huff and puff and blow their houses down.

Since that time, I have had many personal encounters where the "Big Bad Wolf" has shown up in my life at the door of my heart and mind, huffing, puffing, and trying to blow me down. Just like the pigs, when he appeared, I had a false sense of security and did not recognize he was present. But, I quickly became aware of his existence after feeling the hostile winds of adversity he blew into my life. As a result of the damage and devastation, I became apprehensive regarding making a move towards progress. I felt hesitant in my ability to make decisions regarding the direction for my life. I felt intimidated by others who appeared to have it all or were seemingly able to do it all. I felt discouraged by my self-perceived inability to find and pursue my purpose. I felt panic-stricken at the thought of living the rest of my days on earth in this pit. In essence, I felt the paralyzing impact of *fear*.

I recall an experience where fear's grip had consumed my life and left me in a debilitating stupor. I knew that I could not go backwards, but I was too afraid to move forward. I had been offered advice from others which suggested I should "just get over it" to "move on with life."

But the weakening blows of fear had beaten me into a catatonic state that kept me in extreme dysfunction.

However, in the midst of my quandary from this incapacitating experience, this one question came to my mind: "What would you do if you weren't afraid?" In other words, if you were not allowing fear to rule your life, what awesome things could you really accomplish for the purpose for which you were created?

What would you do if fear were not a factor? What goal would you reach? What next step would you take? What unfinished task would you complete? What career would you pursue? What healthy relationships would you attract? What unhealthy relationships would you let go? What doors of opportunities would you walk through? What doors of failure would you close? What final decisions would you make? What direction would you follow? What conversations would you have? What would you walk away from?

Know this, fear keeps us from doing three things. It keeps us from really knowing who we are. It keeps us from walking in faith. It keeps us from using our gifts and pursuing our purpose. Fear impacts our ability to move from where we are to where we have the desire to be. It keeps us stuck in patterns and in the mundane and monotonous. It keeps us living in habits that are not conducive to our well-being. It locks us inside ourselves, mutes our sound, and ultimately turns off our power.

For all of these reasons, you cannot afford to stay there! I know you cannot wave a magic wand and make fear disappear. However, you can change the way you address fear when it shows up in your life. You do not have to submit to its dysfunction and the paralysis it brings. Fear is an emotion. However, your emotional intelligence can outweigh its impact when you position your voice with power and influence.

Voice Positioning Points for FEAR

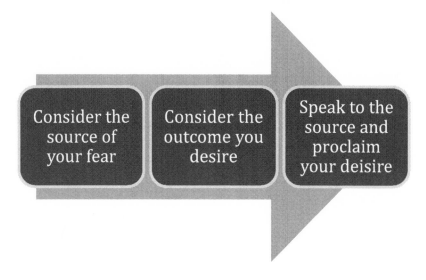

Voice Positioning Point One: Consider the Source of your Fear

Oftentimes we allow fear to exist in our lives without ever inquiring as to where the fear is coming from. What's behind the fear? What is its source? Think about it this way. If you wake up every day with headache, are you going to resolve that having a headache every day is just your plight in life? Or, are you going to make every effort to get to the bottom of what is causing it? I would venture to say that you are going to do everything within your power to alleviate your pain. Why would you not go to the same lengths to alleviate your fear? It's time to consider the source!

Voice Positioning Point Two: Consider the Outcome You Desire

What would your situation or circumstance look like if you removed fear as a factor? Fear can remain and even become stronger until you rise above it to envision your life in the absence of it. This means you must see yourself conquering the perceived limitations fear has convinced you to give in to. More importantly, it means no longer allowing fear to hide in the background while you blame other people, places, and things for the reasons why you are not moving, not shifting, and/or not positioning your authentic voice. It's time to consider the outcome you want!

Voice Positioning Point Three: Speak to the Source and Proclaim Your Desire

Your fear will never move until you speak to it. This will take every aspect (100%) of your authentic voice to address the source. While this includes speaking to your fear out loud (7%), it also includes your actions (93%). In other words, everything that is a part of you speaks. You change your language from fear to faith. You adjust your attitude from defeat to victory. You replace your demeanor from downcast to confidence. Fear cannot remain when your authentic voice becomes stronger. Proclaim what you desire. It's time!

Time For A Change

In a discussion with a young woman, I asked, "What is an area or some areas in your life where you have seen the greatest change occur?" After pondering my inquiry for a few moments, she began to share. She stated that she had spent most of her adult life in the business of pleasing other people. She talked about her concern regarding how they felt about her, what they thought about her, and even how she could get them to care more about her. As a result, she had begun to take drastic measures to adapt herself to what she believed others wanted and expected. She changed the way she looked. She changed the way she dressed. She changed her behavior, not because she was comfortable with these changes, but because she wholeheartedly believed that these changes were necessary to please others.

As I listened intently, I could literally feel hurt rise up in my heart. I could feel my breath grow short. I could feel my eyes fill with tears. All of the sudden, her story had become my own. As she poured out from her soul, I was drawn back to a time when my life mirrored all that she was describing.

I remembered a time when I made changes in my life that were in opposition to who and what God created me to be. I traded in my well-being to try to accommodate someone else. I traded in my self-awareness and opened myself up to receive messages from someone else telling me who I was. I traded in my sense of divine security for trying to find security in another person and the things that came with that person. I traded in my peace in my effort to try to keep the peace. I traded in other meaningful relationships in an effort to be possessed solely by another. I traded in my happiness in an effort to keep another happy. I traded in my joy because I believed I didn't really need it as long as the other person maintained it.

I traded, and I traded, and I traded. I traded to the degree that one day I woke up, and all of me was gone. I had willingly been taken captive by the desires of another and had voluntarily placed myself in a hostage situation. When I came to my senses, my first questions were, "Who am I, and how did I get here?" In fact, these questions were the beginning of my journey out of an enslaved mind. In the words of one of my favorite authors, Charlet Lewis from her book, "I Had to Change" – I HAD TO CHANGE! My authentic voice was depending on it.

Can you relate? Raise your hand right where you are if you've traded in your authentic voice in an effort to please others? You're paying a high price for it, aren't you? Let me answer that for you. Yes, you are. Even if you don't realize it. In fact, that's what your life has been trying to tell you. The price is too high, and the long-term outcome is not good. Something has got to change.

From The Research

As it related to self-sabotaging her authentic voice for the sake of people-pleasing, here is what one of my research study participants had to say: "The reason why I don't speak is because I know it'll probably hurt someone's feelings and I don't want that to be the reason why I speak. I don't want to speak so that it hurts someone. I want to be that individual that leads a change, but sometimes in order to do that you have to make people uncomfortable, but I don't know how, and that's something that's personal. I don't like to hurt people. "The impact for me has been my lack of confidence but also a feeling of being complacent because I'm not really confident that I can do anything else now."

Although this research study participant was in a leadership position, she found it very difficult to lead herself in positioning her authentic voice. She rationalized her choice by creating an internal narrative that caused her to believe that her words would hurt others or make them uncomfortable. It is important to remember that although words have the power to hurt others, our unspoken words have greater power to hurt us. Our bottled-up expressions can sit inside of us for so long, they begin to decay and form toxins that are deadly to our spirit, soul, and body. We convince ourselves that being quiet and just letting it go is the best way – the right way. When, in actuality, our unwillingness to confront others is a manifestation of our unwillingness to confront ourselves.

Voice Action: Okay. Get really honest with yourself right now. In what ways is the "disease to please" showing up in your life? I know it is not our goal to displease anyone. However, you will not please everyone. So, ask yourself these questions: *What am I really afraid of? What do I believe I will lose if I speak up? Will I really lose that? What is the worst thing that can happen? What is the best thing that can happen? What am I willing to risk for the sake of my authentic voice? What am I willing to change?*

_____

_____

_____

_____

_____

_____

"The Authentic Voice Assessment Model"

During my doctoral studies, I created a model for personal reflection and change, *The Authentic Voice Assessment Model*. This model is designed to serve as a tool for assessing your voice journey through exploring what your voice has been, what your voice is now, and what your voice is becoming. The model provides a framework for you to learn from your past voice lessons, to understand the voice capacity you have now, and to envision the power of your voice for your future. It is a model for discovery and change.

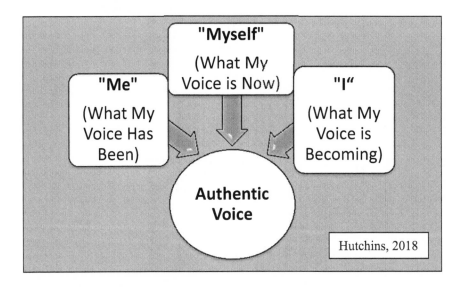

"Me" – What My Voice Has Been

In the previous section of the book, *Knowing Your Voice (Voice Authenticity)*, you took a deep dive into coming face-to-face with and acknowledging who you have been. You were able to get a glimpse of how your voice journey began. However, more than reflecting on the journey, you had the opportunity to find the "How" and the "Why" of your voice identity. You were able to discover how you learned to mask your authentic voice and why you "caged" it. This work was critical because attempting to move forward without unearthing the artifacts of where you've been will not serve you well on your voice journey.

As such, the "Me" component of the *Authentic Voice Assessment Model* calls for deeper reflection and exploration. More specifically, now that you understand some of the ways in which your authentic voice has been covered or hidden, you can now tell yourself the truth about what your voice has been and the impact on your life.

Voice Action: "<u>Me</u>" – Here is the place to acknowledge what your voice has been. Don't dress up your description. It is here where your naked truth is warranted. *Consider your past and the lessons you've learned, messages about voice others have passed down through generations, voice rules that were imposed on you, and most importantly, what you believed. Identify the parts of your past voice narrative that you are ready and willing to change in an effort to reclaim your authentic voice:*

_____

_____

_____

_____

_____

_____

"Myself" – What My Voice Is Now

Now that you have done the work in looking back, I want you to answer a few questions, honestly and transparently about where you are right now:

1. What baggage have you brought from your past that you need to unpack right now?
2. How is this baggage influencing how you show up in the world now?
3. How is this baggage getting in your way?

Speaking metaphorically, imagine carrying around bags you packed 10, 20, or 30+ years ago. Imagine the weight of those bags and the impact of carrying that weight over time.

As a part of an exercise in a women's class I was teaching, I asked for two volunteers. Two women bravely came to the front, unsure of what was about to take place. I asked the women if they would consent to running a race a few laps around the perimeter of our classroom. They both agreed. However, before I gave them the starting alert, I handed one of the women three bags. One bag had a strap and was placed on her shoulder. She held the other two bags in her hands. After she was situated with what she had been given, I marked a starting point and communicated the standard, "On your mark...get set...go!"

Both women began running as the others in the class cheered them on. Approximately thirty seconds into the run, the woman with no bags was running with ease. She was showing no signs of fatigue and apparently had plenty of energy to keep going. However, the woman with the three bags was already in trouble. She had fallen behind and could no longer keep up with the other woman. Her breathing was labored, and on many occasions, she looked as if she was going to drop all she was carrying. At the point when her struggle really began to get the best of her, she began asking me, "Can I stop now?" My response was, "No, keep going." After the seventh lap, I asked both of them to stop.

The woman with no bags slowly came to a halt, a little winded, but smiling nevertheless. However, as soon as I said "stop," the woman carrying the bags dropped them immediately and reached for a chair to sit down to catch her breath. While she rested, I asked the first woman about her experience running the race. She stated that the race had been fun for her. She enjoyed the excitement and the encouragement from the others in the class. Even when she got tired, it helped her to hear the cheers of the others, and it gave her the motivation to keep going.

Conversely, when I asked the other woman about her experience, she stated that it was more difficult than she had expected. Running with the bags impacted her in ways she never would have imagined. She stated that not only was she tired but also, she really was not mindful of the cheers from the others in the class because she was so preoccupied by the discomfort she was experiencing while focusing on not dropping her bags. She also stated that she grew impatient with me because no matter how many times she asked if she could stop, I said no. It was as if I was fully aware of her struggle and simply chose to ignore it.

After hearing her comments, I asked her to open each one of her bags. She was amazed by what she found. Inside each bag was a ten-pound weight. She had been trying to run her race carrying weight. What was more interesting, during the time she was running her race, she only asked if she could quit. She never asked if she could lay her bags down.

The parallels to our voice journey are clear. We are to proceed freely and without hindrances. However, when we begin to take on things that weigh us down, our race is drastically affected. We become tired and begin to lose our focus. Because of the pressure mentally, physically, and emotionally, we become disengaged and we lose motivation. We also become frustrated and irritated with the ones around us who are encouraging us to keep moving forward. We feel as if it's easy for them to say, they don't feel what we feel, and they are not carrying what we are carrying. Instead of helping us, they are really being insensitive to our plight. Right? Wrong!

The real solution is to simply lay your bags down! Honestly! How far are you going to be able to go with the weight you are carrying? The answer is, not far. In fact, you may be at your limit as you are reading these words. When you choose to hang on to weights, you choose to sabotage your own voice success. In essence, you make this voice race virtually impossible to win.

Voice Action: "MYSELF" – Here is the place to acknowledge what your voice is now. If the weight of any person, place or thing is hidden in bags you are carrying, now is the opportunity to determine what you are going to do with the weight. Are you going to continue in your fatigued state of being? Or, are you ready to drop your bags so you can move freely on your journey? *If you chose freedom, then name your weight. Go ahead! Confront every heavy thing you have been dragging around and continue to* *drag now. This will require your brutal honesty. Step into the courage to tell yourself the truth. Once you have your list, describe how the things you are dragging around are ultimately dragging you down. The lower you go, the more your authentic voice is minimized. What are you willing to do with these weights in order to reclaim your authentic voice?*

_____

_____

_____

_____

_____

_____

"I" – What My Voice Is Becoming

I was having a conversation with a woman I met at the conclusion of a keynote presentation I had just given. During my presentation, I talked about the fact that living our authentic voice requires a commitment to moving out of fear and walking by faith. Stirred by what she heard, she waited at the back of the room until the majority of the other attendees had departed. She approached me eagerly and grabbed my hand. She shared with me an encounter that had shifted her life from the grips of fear to experiencing the power of faith.

She told me a few years ago she decided to take a cruise. At one of the stops along her voyage, she had an opportunity to take a tour into a tropical rain forest. Although she was extremely apprehensive because of the unknown, she was determined to take the tour anyway. When her group arrived at the destination to begin the tour, horrific fear overwhelmed her. All she could see was a monstrosity of trees, a never-ending sea of vines, and a backdrop of every other piece of greenery imaginable. She wondered how they would ever find their way, how they would ever get through to the other side, and about all the wildlife that could possibly be lying in wait for them in anticipation of their next meal. Even so, she wanted to stay committed to the choice she made before leaving the comforts of her luxurious cruise ship.

The journey began. They entered in under what seemed to be a leafy canopy hanging over their heads. It was extremely difficult to see ahead or know what turn or direction they were going to take next. This was nerve-wracking for her because everything in her mind wanted to see the plan and anticipate what was to come. Yet, she could not. This was not her tour, and she was not the one in control. Actually, her not being in total control was what frightened her the most.

Nevertheless, in the midst of her anxiety and her dread for even consenting to this excursion in the first place, she recognized something. She recognized that she did not have to know the direction. She did not have to know the next turn. She did not have to know where the tour was going to lead her. She realized they were in the hands of a very capable tour guide. For this reason, she knew she did not have to have all the answers. Her only responsibility was to trust the process and enjoy the trip.

The journey to reclaiming and positioning your authentic voice may be a scary one for you. Based upon where your voice has been and where it is now, you may not be able to fathom what your voice has the possibility to become. Well, here is the beauty of your voice journey; you don't have to know. You don't have to have it all figured out. Faith requires your trust.

Trust in this context means you surrender the things you are holding on to that haven't served you well. It means you relinquish control. It means you address the things about your voice that scare you. Doing so will help you not to shrink back and hide your voice because others fear it. Trust means showing up, knowing you are fully equipped to honor your truth.

Trust what? I'm glad you asked…trust your authentic voice. This is the place of your power and influence. It is from here that you advance to new levels of confidence and evolution of your voice journey.

Voice Action: "I" – Here is the place where you dare to dream about what your voice is becoming. This is the time you invite your mind, your heart, and your spirit to align in a way that allows you to envision the power and influence you will have as you position your voice for positive impact. *Consider what it will feel like and what it will look like. Consider those you will influence. Consider the ways your authentic voice will change the environment around you. Consider the positive impact on the culture of which you are a part. As your voice is becoming all that it is becoming, consider how free you will be to boldly and confidently live in your voice authenticity. Now, write what you see. Write your vision:*

_____

_____

_____

_____

_____

_____

I am certain you have figured out by now that trusting the authentic voice inside of you is the key to your voice freedom. In fact, your trust is the driver of the entire process. In truth, you will never be able to harness your power and master your influence without trusting that your authentic voice is the most precious gift you have, and its value is an asset to the world. The absence of this trust will diminish your confidence and cause your authentic voice to become muted even if you are the one muting it. Take a lesson from the research.

From The Research

A research study participant shared her perceptions and experiences of her own silence in the organization where she worked. She highlighted ways in which the power interwoven into systems served to fuel organizational dynamics that led to her silence. With great confidence and strength of voice prior to coming to the organization, over time she was met with systemic realities in leadership, structure, and expectations that ultimately served to mute her voice and generated feelings of "pulling back." Communicating her frustration with being silent, she expressed feeling embarrassed and ashamed as she shared her loss of confidence and how her silence had caused her to no longer be herself.

The Betrayal

You see, sitting in silence when your authentic voice is screaming on the inside of you to get out, can be torture. This sense of "suffering in silence" drains your confidence as eats away at the core of who you are.

I distinctly remember those days of working in an organization where silence was embedded in the culture. No one on the team spoke up to leadership. Instead, conversations happened in the form of whispers, or in conversations after work, or in text messages during the course of the day. The agony of having truth locked on the inside was unbearable. The energy it took to avoid the "elephant" in the organization was sickening. The surface way of relating was hypocritical. Monday through Friday, day-in and day-out, this silence was deafening. Although the weekend brought some reprieve, Sunday evening brought with it the knots in my gut, knowing I had to return to a place where my authentic voice was not invited, was not valued and was not honored.

Over time, I grew very distrusting of my environment. However, what I did not realize was that my distrust was stemming from the distrust of my own voice. This distrust arose from my own self-betrayal. I had failed to honor, protect, guard, and maintain its authenticity. I had become unfaithful to myself.

Nevertheless, I blamed others. I convinced myself that if they were kinder, gentler, more sensitive, caring, and loving, I would speak up. I would address some things. I would give it my all. But, the truth of the matter is, while I was giving all of my attention to the external relationships around me, I was neglecting everything on the inside of me that desperately needed me. You see, when you are unfaithful to yourself, you don't show-up for you. You are emotionally divided, your focus shifts, you turn your back on your power and influence, and trust is broken.

Because trust is seated at the core of every healthy relationship, when we don't trust our authentic voice, it compromises the health of the relationship between our mind and our spirit. The burden associated with this disharmony is a heavy one. We stop opening ourselves and we lose transparency.

Fixing What's Broken

The first step in rebuilding trust is to acknowledge you have broken it in the first place. It is about taking responsibility for your actions and accepting the consequences. You must embrace the process of restoring whatever has been damaged or destroyed. It means you will have to do the following:

1. Believe your relationship with your authentic voice is worth saving.
2. Forgive yourself for all the ways you've neglected your authentic voice.
3. Make peace with the things that are behind you.
4. Commit to doing the work it will take to restore what was lost.

Voice Action: Trusting will take time. It will also require practice. *Consider what you will do to build trust in your authentic voice. What opportunities will you take to be bold? In what ways will you stand in your confidence?*

_____

_____

_____

_____

_____

_____

Once trust is lost, it is not easily regained. I can't count the number of times my clients have shared with me their experiences of losing trust. Whether in a marriage, a friendship, a workplace, or even in a faith community, the devastation of navigating distrust was central to how they moved about in the world. For example, one client shared, "I quickly cut people if I get the slightest inkling that I cannot trust them. So, I don't have a lot of people in my circle because I've learned to cut quickly."

We learn to "cut people" out of our lives. However, cutting can really hurt. Yes, there are people who need to be gone. But, there are also people that need to stay... even when it's a challenge having them there. We need them because they have something to teach us. They are the ones who have a role in helping us to skillfully position our voice. When you trust the power of your authentic voice, you don't have to "cut" others, you merely reposition them in your life. Doing so allows you to not be broken by them, instead you can break the power of their actions hovering over you.

Voice Positioning Points for TRUST

| Trust the voice of your past | Trust the voice of your present | The the voice of your future |

Voice Positioning Point One: Trust the Process From Your Past

Trust that whatever you have lived through in your past has given you the opportunity to use the lessons learned as the evolutionary history for your authentic voice. Even if your past was filled with bad and ugly issues, there are still priceless nuggets from those experiences that can help strengthen you today. So, don't be apprehensive about looking back over your past. Go ahead and reflect so you can grab what you need for your journey. Nothing you have walked though was a waste. Now is the time to position it. Your life stories have great power. Don't allow any secrets to hold your authentic voice hostage because you have been guilty or ashamed. Whatever your voice has been can now be used as building blocks for what it is becoming. Trust the process.

Voice Positioning Point Two: Trust the Process In Your Present

When you recognize the power of your past, you can infuse that power into your present. This does not mean that you have gotten your authentic voice all together, it means you are committed to standing in what you know as you keep posturing yourself to learn. It is here where you determine you will not allow past failure, hurt, disappointment, and the like, to interfere with your future. This is the place where you decide you are not going back and you begin to look ahead to determine how you will move forward. In the process, you embrace every moment of your now. You become mindful of the moments you have. It is here where you craft what you want your authentic voice message to the world to be. This is the place where you trust the power of your authentic voice to create an amazing future. Trust the process.

Voice Positioning Point Three: Trust the Process For Your Future

Proverbs 18:21 reminds us, "Life and death are in the power of the tongue." One of the greatest gifts of your authentic voice is the power to speak life! This means you are able to speak life-giving things to yourself and to others. This is also the process by which you begin to speak your heart's desire for your future. This is where you begin to position your authentic voice, not just for where you are, but for where you're going. It is here where you speak your affirmation of who you are, your purpose, your destiny, and your heart's desires. It is here where you position your authentic voice to frame the personal world you envision for your future. It is here where you recognize the power of your authentic voice to change everything. Trust the process.

My Hope For You…

Okay! You've made it through chapter one and you've almost completed chapter two of this book. You've done a lot of digging, reflecting and discovering. Perhaps, this is not what you thought you would be doing when you picked up this book. Nevertheless, I am delighted you have committed and stayed the course. Congratulations! I hope you gained a good sense of who and what to trust in your life. I hope you have learned what to do with fear. I hope you were able to assess your authentic voice through your reflection on your past, present, and future. I hope you committed to fixing the broken parts of your authentic voice. Most importantly, I hope you learned the value of trusting your authentic voice and positioning it with confidence.

TAKE YOUR POSITION!

Trusting your voice is the foundation for confidence. Before you proceed to the next section of the book, you must take your position:

1. **Stand in Your Authentic Voice** – Because your authentic voice is unique to you, there is nothing about it that compares to someone else's. It is never inferior to another person's voice. It is the container of your truth and it is the representation of your presence in the world. It is the purest gift you can give away. It is what you came in the world with. It is the legacy you will leave behind. Your authentic voice opens up spaces you wish to occupy. It creates the path to access the answers to your prayers. It frames your life. It is the portal to sustaining your peace, joy, and love. It is the strong foundation upon which you stand. Engage your authentic voice for bold positioning. You've got this!

2. **Harness Your Power** – You have a powerful voice history. Use the lessons from your history to help you navigate your present and to help you envision your future. Doing so will require you to not waiver in trusting your authentic voice. Even when you are faced with unknowns, proceed with confidence and power in knowing your authenticity will keep you steady and focused. You've got this!

3. **Master Your Influence** – When you trust your authentic voice and you stand boldly and confidently in your truth, you influence others to do the same. Be mindful of the power you have and position that power in a way that impacts every place your feet take you, everything your hands touch, every idea your mind can conceive, and every dream your heart can fathom. You've got this!

MY VOICE COMMITMENT LETTER

Dear _____

Today, I commit to:

_____

_____

_____

_____

_____

_____

_____

_____

_____

_____

Love,

_____

CHAPTER THREE

Creating Space for Your Voice (Voice Visibility)

CHAPTER THREE
Creating Space for Your Voice (Voice Visibility)

If it doesn't exist, create it! That's how powerful spaces are made. ~Dr. K

I am so excited for you to begin this chapter. Since you've made it here, I believe you have done the work to get here! I know the process may have been a bit tedious. However, gathering and taking out the garbage is rarely a pleasant experience. Especially, when you have to sort through it first. But, my hope is that you have deep discoveries about your voice. In fact, jot down some notes about what you've learned so far:

_____

_____

_____

_____

_____

_____

_____

_____

Although, I cannot see what you've written in your notes, here are some "power" words I hope showed up:

These words are the fabric of your voice journey. They are a beautiful tapestry of power, interwoven into your voice identity. As you move forward through the pages ahead, you will continue to make discoveries that will characterize your voice evolution. Here is the next one for your consideration – SPACE!

What's Space Got to Do With It?

Pause for a moment and consider how cluttered life can become. Consider all the things that are on your to-do list. Think about your daily routine and all the tasks, responsibilities, and obligations that fill your days. Like a drawer, a closet, a desk, a house, our lives get cluttered. They become filled with monotonous mundane routines. We spread ourselves all over the place. When we do, we clutter our way.

We also clutter our lives with things we have not let go of. Think about it. What garment are you still holding on to because you keep telling yourself one day you are going to be able to wear it again? However, it's been 15 years. Just like that garment, there are other things we hold on to that will never fit us again. We hold on to people we have outgrown. We hold on to places we have outgrown. We hold on to things we have outgrown. In fact, pause here and think about the people, places, and things you know for sure you have outgrown yet you are still holding on to them. Write it down:

_____

_____

_____

_____

_____

_____

_____

_____

_____

I often ask the clients I have the opportunity to coach this question, "What would be the best thing about letting go?" Many have challenges answering this question because they have become hoarders. No, I am not being harsh. I am being honest. The truth of the matter is, you may be a hoarder too. As a point of clarity, in this context I am referring to the things you've accumulated, and you've kept in your life-space, yet these things are serving no real purpose. You are just keeping them. So, let's check. You know you are a hoarder if:

- *failed relationships* are keeping you from the possibility of a good one
- *traditions* of "how it's always been done" keeps you in a rut doing it that way
- *betrayal* of a friend causes you to quickly cut others from your life
- *lowered self-esteem* keeps getting in your way because someone once said you were not enough
- *unforgiveness* of a person who caused you hurt keeps you hurting
- *anger* toward a system who failed to recognize your value has made you bitter
- *rejection* of your love for someone has gotten in the way of you loving others

While I can keep going on and on with the, "you know you are a hoarder if" list, I wanted to give you a glimpse of real scenarios of the things many of those I have coached were holding on to. Now, did you see your "stuff" amongst the rubble of (check all that apply):

- _____failed relationship
- _____traditions
- _____betrayal
- _____lowered-self esteem
- _____unforgiveness
- _____anger
- _____rejection

What is the story connected to the items you checked? If the story is not one where you have conquered or overcome, that means you are hoarding the negative emotions attached to what happened. That also means that whatever you are holding on to has cluttered your life. The thing about clutter is...things get lost in it...things like your authentic voice.

Clearing the Clutter

I have watched the reality show *Hoarders*. Each episode depicts the lives of individuals who are in crisis and are living in homes where they are nearly buried in things they have accumulated over time and are unable to part with. There is always an intervention from family members, friends, or neighbors as a last attempt to try to help the individuals before other drastic measures are taken.

Well, this is your intervention. I am serving you notice that it's time to clear the clutter. You can no longer walk around holding on to things that are filling up your space and blocking the blessings that would ultimately come to you if you had enough room to receive them. Just like nothing can get in, your authentic voice can't get out because your other "stuff" is piled on top of it. Therefore, whatever you are giving out in the world is what you are most full of.

Why Hold On?

I know it is easy for me to say just let go. It's right up there with the adage "easier said than done." Please know I am not suggesting it is easy. In fact, I understand some reasons why we hold on. We hold on because whatever we are holding is familiar and we are comfortable with it. Holding on becomes our security blanket. We hold on because there are great risks associated with letting go. We hold on because we are not accustomed to being vulnerable and we fear what letting go might bring. We simply don't want to open ourselves up to the unknown. Why should we when we get along just fine the way we are? But, is the way you are, and the way things are really serving you well?

Holding on and hoarding minimizes your authentic voice. It leaves you discombobulated and unable to get clear. It leaves you void of direction and lacking in energy to make power decisions for your life. As a result, you create internal spaces that are not conducive to your well-being and you allow yourself to remain in external spaces where you are not able to harness your power or master your influence. This causes you to lose sight of the value of freeing up your space.

Voice Action: Is your internal and external world filled with so much clutter right now that it's hard for you to get a sense of direction? Are you struggling to get clear about the next steps to take? Do you have things you want to say and do but you don't know how to even begin? Is your authentic voice lost underneath it all? If you answered yes to any or all of these questions, it is critical that you clear the clutter. Your authentic voice will never be able to shine through if it has to compete with the accumulation of things in and around you. So, let me ask you... What would letting go and clearing the clutter look like for you? Who would it be? What would it be? Why is it necessary? What difference would it make in your life?

_____

_____

_____

_____

_____

_____

This is the part of your voice journey where you give yourself permission to address and/or dismiss anything from your life that keeps you in a state of accumulating, hoarding, and cluttering. This is the place where you recognize the value of creating a space where you can position your authentic voice in powerful and impactful ways. This is the place where you master your influence and you begin to include your voice instead of allowing it to get lost, or not heard, or not seen. This is the place of urgency. If you don't clear this clutter in your space, it has the potential to bury you alive.

From The Research

Accepting the realities of their silence, the study participants' responses to interview questions revealed that while they entered into their organizations with a willingness and ability to speak, they became silent or were silenced as a result of systemic barriers to voice. Encumbered by the self-imposed limitations to speak or by systems that were not conducive to soliciting their voices, the participants realized the mental and emotional noise that cluttered their spaces that led to their day-to-day silence in the workplace.

Voice Positioning Points for SPACE

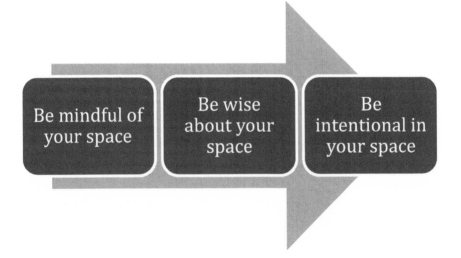

Be mindful of your space

Be wise about your space

Be intentional in your space

Voice Positioning Point One: Be Mindful of Your Space

Positioning your authentic voice will require that you are mindful of your space at all times. This means that you are increasingly aware of your surroundings. This means you are consistently assessing where and how to place your authentic voice. It is here where you are sensitive to the moment-by-moment movement and happenings in your life. You observe your own processes and the processes of others. You are awakened and alive to opportunities to be positively impactful with your presence and powerful with your influence. Be mindful of your space.

Voice Positioning Point Two: Be Wise About Your Space

Positioning your authentic voice in your space will require your wisdom. It is here where you must consider who and what to allow in and who and what to clear out. This is where you do the math in your life. If any person, place, or thing is subtracting from you instead of adding to you, then you must change the equation. Keeping your space healthy is too critical to not have keen discernment and sound judgment concerning it. Be vigilant in setting and keeping boundaries. Be unapologetic regarding the boundaries you set. Be wise about your space.

Voice Positioning Point Three: Be Intentional In Your Space

There is nothing more powerful than waking up each day with an intention to be deliberate and purposeful in your space. It is here where you no longer leave your life to chance, but instead, you create space in the world where you can flourish and thrive. It is here where you resolve how you will influence those around you and the world. Being intentional about your space means you live your life on ready – always postured for the good things to come. Be intentional in your space.

Don't Get Lost in the Noise

I was having lunch with my two-year-old niece and my mother. As usual, my niece had been extremely busy and continued to busy herself as we waited for the food we ordered to arrive. It was the peak of the lunch hour, and the restaurant was full of customers. The servers scurried about taking and delivering orders. People were finishing up and leaving, tables were cleaned, and new customers were seated.

With constant movement around us, my niece played with crayons, her menu, forks, spoons, saltshakers, peppershakers, and anything else that she could get her hands on. In the middle of her multitasking with all the items she had gathered, she stopped in somewhat of a frozen position, leaned her head to the side and in an instant asked, "What's that sound?" Curious as to what she was hearing, I asked, "What sound?" She pointed up in the air and said, "That sound." I was oblivious to what she meant, so I paused for a moment to listen more intently. All of a sudden, I realized the sound she was referring to was the sound of music playing overhead in the restaurant. I told her the sound she heard was music, and she asked, "Music?" My response was "Yes, music." She said "okay" and went back to her play.

What I found fascinating about this whole ordeal was the analogy I drew to our authentic voice journey. Noise surrounds us in the activities of everyday living. We are busy playing with all the items we have brought to our life's table, including spouses, children, friends, jobs, and so on. Yet, in the midst of it all, do we stop what we are doing and ask, "What's that sound?" On the other hand, do we even realize there is a sound in the background at all?

From The Research

Participants in the research admitted to having feelings of being isolated and uninvited when faced with silence in the organizations where they each worked. Related to feeling isolated, one participant shared, "I think sometimes silence looks like being in a room by yourself and with the idea that nobody else is with you, that you're all alone, that you're very isolated and that nobody else gets it. Nobody else. You don't have anybody to lean on. You don't have anybody who's got you by the hand saying, 'We can do this.' I do think that sometimes silence, can feel very isolating." Another participant shared her feelings related to feeling uninvited. "There is now a very clear bifurcation of who has a voice and who doesn't in the big decisions. I came up with a term last year; I feel like myself and my colleagues, those of us who are at mid- level managers of my institution, we are simply white noise."

Oftentimes, the noise can be so loud it is deafening. As a result, we stop hearing it. However, we are still influenced by it. Think about it this way. Have you ever listened to a song on the radio and perhaps even sang along with it; yet, when the song was over, and still hours later, you found yourself humming it? That is the power of noise in our life. It lingers with us and influences us in ways that compromise our authentic voice because we begin to normalize the noise and minimize our voice. However, going along with the noise, should not be the norm.

Voice Action: What noise is filling your world? This noise could be in the organizations, institutions, or systems you're in. This noise might be coming from the voices of others. It could be the complaining and whispering happening around you. It could be the opinions and feelings of others. The noise could even be the silence of others. The noise may be your own silence. The noise can come from your family, friends, relationships, workplaces, and places of worship. Reflect on where you are in your life right now. *Assess where there is noise and where it is coming from:*

_____

_____

_____

_____

_____

_____

No Dumping Allowed

As you completed your personal assessment, chances are you recognized all the ways the noise coming from others has cluttered your space. Yes, you filled your space. However, you have probably allowed others to dump in your space as well.

During a Saturday excursion with my mother, we decided to go into one of our favorite fast-food restaurants to have a chicken sandwich for lunch. We ordered, took our seats, engaged in good conversation, and began eating our meal. While we were sitting there, one of the employees came and began the process of replacing a trash bag in a nearby receptacle that had been filled to overflowing. After struggling for a few seconds to free the bulging bag, she loaded it onto a cart, put a fresh bag in the receptacle, and took the old trash away. My mother and I completed our meals and prepared to leave. I gathered my trash and my mother's trash, piled it all on one tray, dumped it into the new trash bag, and headed out to continue our activities.

After that day, I gave no further thought to that particular event until most recently. I was having a conversation with a young woman who works in ministry. She talked about the fatigue she was beginning to experience as a result of listening to the cares, problems, concerns, issues, situations, and circumstances of others.

At first, she took pleasure in hearing information and offering her advice and guidance. She believed that she was offering godly wisdom and sound teaching that would motivate these individuals toward positive results. However, after a period of time, something began to happen.

Many of the people with whom she was sharing her knowledge, instruction, and personal experiences were consistently coming back to her without having made any movement or action toward obtaining positive results. Upon questioning these individuals regarding what had been discussed during their times of counsel, she found that they had done absolutely nothing with the information she had shared. However, many of them were still coming back to her for more.

Sensing her extreme frustration, I immediately recalled the events that transpired at lunch that day with my mother. It seems that just like the trash bag the young woman in the restaurant struggled with, this young woman was struggling with her own metaphorical trash bag. It had been filled to capacity, and she literally felt she had no room to receive anything else. Not only was her bag filled to the point of bursting, but the same people that had been responsible for filling it were still coming back to put more on top of what had already been deposited. What's worse, none of these "depositors" in this young woman's life had given any thought to what was happening to their trash after they dumped it on her.

For many of us, it is time to put up a "No Dumping" sign over our personal receptacles. It is not in our best interest, nor does it enhance our overall well-being, for us to continue to accept the rubbish brought to us by others. We are not shutting down to hearing the legitimate concerns of those who want to move forward, see a change, and go to the next level. However, we are closing the doors to those who are just looking for someone on which to dump.

Voice Action: *Who are you allowing to "dump" on you time-and-time again? How has this impacted your sense of well-being? What is keeping you from saying "no" and protecting your space? What are you willing to change? Why do you want to change it? What do you expect to see from the change?*

_____

_____

_____

_____

_____

Have A Vision for Your Space

I am a big fan of HGTV. I love watching the shows where they take homes that look like they should be completely demolished and work to restore them to a thing of beauty. I am always in awe of the transformation from deplorable to dazzling. The most interesting part is the process simply begins with a vision for what the space could be.

Now that you have done a thorough assessment of the condition of your space, it's time to dream big about what you want your space to be. What will a complete redesign look like? What do you want to add to your space that will make it absolutely magnificent? What do you want to reconfigure that will give you more symmetry and alignment? What statement do you want your space to make?

I ask you these questions because you have arrived at a point on your voice journey where you must see your authentic voice differently from the way you have seen it before. You have done powerful work to get to this point and you can now put your expanded knowledge back into spaces that were too cluttered and too small. You are at the point where you allow your vision for your space to become more powerful than the reality of your space. You only need to see what it will be so that you can remain encouraged and inspired until it gets there. Also, know this... the vision you have for your space does not require anyone else to see. Your vision only requires you.

Tear the Walls Down

On the HGTV shows, after they envision what the space has the potential to be, they begin the process with tearing down anything that is not a part of the vision. They tear down structures that are not needed. They never begin with what the house needs on the outside. They always begin the process on the inside.

Walls come down from the inside. Your authentic voice journey is an inside job. It is about creating the space you need on the inside, so your authentic voice has a safe and healthy place to live and thrive. For this reason, there are things that must come down.

This is where you harness the power of your authentic voice and you take control of your space. This is where you commit to creating more open space for your life. You determine to create a space where more light can come in and there is better flow. This is where you address the structures, systems, and barriers to your authentic voice. This is the place where you step into the courage to tear down and break apart the very thing that has been breaking you.

From The Research

Certain of the power of her voice, one research participant approached the balance between silence and voice behaviors with a sense of control. Recognizing her ability to determine when and how she would position her voice, she was able to compartmentalize the feelings of frustration, pain, anxiety, and anger connected to perpetual silence. With the desire for the health of the organization and for her own sense of well-being, the participant was driven by needing to make the choice to position her voice. Thus, her commitment to voice became the means by which she included herself in organizational conversations and decision-making. Managing feelings of intimidation related to speaking up, the participant became a contributor to organizational dialogue, even when the invitation was not extended to do so.

Be A Disruptor

I was waiting in line in a department store. There were a few people in front of me. Standing at the register was a young woman with a little girl who appeared to be about two years-old. While waiting to complete check-out, the little girl kept asking for an item. The young woman kept ignoring her requests. The little girl kept asking. On what seemed to be about the fifth time, the young woman turned to the little girl and said, "If you don't stop that @#%* whining right now, I am going to slap you in your #@*% mouth! Shut-up and I mean it!"

There was complete silence in our check-out line and the surrounding area. It was as if a cloud of "hush" fell in the store. More specifically, the face of the little girl spoke volumes. With her bottom lip quivering, afraid to let out a whimper, her breaths grew fast and shallow. She kept her eyes on the young woman (I believe for fear more might be coming) and dared not move or utter another sound.

I left the store feeling so very sad for the little girl. I thought about how awful the experience was. I could still feel the knot in the pit of my gut. I could not imagine what the little girl's life was like if this was the way she was always spoken to. I could not imagine the impact these kinds of words and tone would ultimately have on her life, her sense of identity, her confidence, and her self-esteem. In my mind it was just awful! Absolutely awful!

Yet, it was not until I really began to delve into this work that I realized something I had not previously considered regarding this story. Everyone in the line and surrounding area became a part of the little girl's silence. As heart-wrenching as it was to watch her be muted, we also muted ourselves along with her. We did absolutely nothing to disrupt the silence. We saw and felt the emotions connected to the silence. But, we did nothing about it.

Pause to consider the detriment of this silence. No, I am not suggesting that silence is always a bad thing (I will talk more about this later in the book). I am speaking specifically of silence that is driven by others. It is the silence that comes as a result of a person, place, or thing assuming dominant power over you. It is forced silence. This silence is fueled by fear and shuts down your authentic voice and renders it dysfunctional. Like an infestation, this type of silence invades your mind, spirit, and body and manifests itself in the following ways…

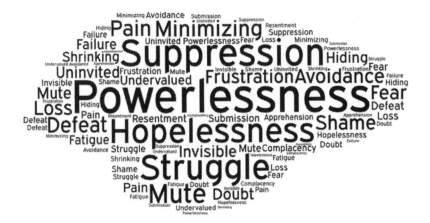

I have coined a term for this type of voice dysfunction, *Traumatic Silence* – that is, the deeply distressing lived experience of silence, brought on by a misuse of power, domination, and intimidation. Traumatic silence happens as a result of intentional muting. The outcome of experiencing *traumatic silence* is what I call, *Post Traumatic Silence Disorder* (PTSD). This condition interrupts healthy, positive, and powerful voice functioning.

The big question is, are you ready to disrupt this silence in your life? Specifically, I am asking if you are willing to interrupt any person, activity, process, structure, or system that is drastically altering and/or destroying your authentic voice? Are you ready to go after your recovery from PTSD? If you are ready and willing, I believe you are able! However, disrupting the silence will require courageous acts on your part. Without these actions, there will be no disruption and no recovery:

1. **Invite Critical Conversations** - These are conversations you have been avoiding. These critical conversations are in reference to issues and situations in your life where you know nothing will change without conversation. However, you have continually made excuses for not having the conversation. You have allowed the elephant to live in the room and you've even fed it like it was your pet. You have even convinced yourself that your silence is simply, "keeping the peace" when you have no peace at all. So, here is my question, what will your life become if you don't have the conversations you need to have? Consider this, critical conversations create healthy space. Although these conversations don't come with an "easy" button, they are the ones that will literally change your life.

2. **Be Okay With Conflict** – You will have conflict when you take action toward disrupting the silence and toward your recovery. This conflict will arise because you will no longer compromise your authentic voice in order to be under the control, domination, opinions, structure, systems, operations, ego, and/or misuse of power from others. If you are going to disrupt the silence and recover, you cannot run from the conflict. Instead, embrace it as a sign of change. Walk into it as an

opportunity to clear your space. It is not about winning. It is about protecting what you value. Keep this truth in mind, you will rarely "win" when you come against what a person believes. The goal is to no longer be oppressed by those beliefs.

3. **Modify Your Style** – As you disrupt the silence and pursue your recovery, you will need to modify your style. No doubt, others have experienced you as submissive to their power. Therefore, you will have to approach disruption and recovery with a different style. This is where you consult your authentic voice and you speak confidently from there. The goal of making space for your voice has to be stronger than the fear of speaking differently. You cannot continue to complain and conform. This is the place where you allow your truth to lead you into elevating your perspective to the degree that it changes your voice in a positive way. You have the power.

4. **Sit On the Table** – Disrupting the silence and recovering is more than merely having "a seat at the table" – It is about sitting on the table. It is about making your presence positive and powerful! It is about allowing how you show up to literally shift the space you enter in a meaningful way. It is about leading with your value, recognizing that others will never recognize your voice while you're at the table if you "undervalue" what you bring to the table. So, put all of you on the table! Show up! Speak up! Stand up! The goal is to no longer be invisible and ignored.

5. **Support Others in Their Disruption and Recovery** – The reality is there will be those who will not listen to you no matter what you do or say. Don't be discouraged by this fact. Recognize your disruption and recovery will model something very powerful and meaningful for others who are longing to disrupt their own silence and have their own recovery. As they watch your journey, they will find the permission they need to pursue their own. When you see it, support it. Disruption and recovery become more powerful when there are others with you and when you are with them.

Voice Action: You have reached the point where you have to be determined to break your silence, disrupt what needs to be disrupted, and pursue your recovery. This is about your choice. This is where no one else is blamed. This is where you take action. Walk yourself through the steps you are going to take. *Why are you taking these steps? What do you expect as an outcome?*

_____

_____

_____

_____

_____

_____

It is your time to stop living by default and start living by design. It is time for you to position your authentic voice in a way that allows you to harness your power, master your influence, and create the space you need and want. It is time for you to own your value and worth and no longer clutter it with junk from sources that have little to no relevance to your journey.

In a conversation with one of my coaching clients, she shared with me all the people who sabotaged her success, all the ones who got it wrong about her value, all the ones that could have advocated for her, but did not, and all the ones who didn't care if she made it or not. I allowed her to go on and on, because I needed her to get that out of her space. When she finished, I asked her one question – "Whose responsibility is it to release all of that?"

My Hope For You...

Creating space for your voice requires your active participation. It is no one else's responsibility to move the things you've hoarded and cluttered your world with. You cannot blame others for your failure to clean up what you own. So, I hope you have come to understand the critical necessity of letting go of what no longer serves a purpose in your life. I hope you have committed to navigating the noise in your life, so you can hear what you need to hear and shut out the distractions. I hope you have stepped into the courage to not allow others to dump on you. I hope you will address the fear related to the fear of disrupting your silence and the silence of others. I hope you are ready to take responsibility for maximizing the space you create. Your authentic voice will thank you for being intentional in giving it a new place to live and thrive. Now breathe...

TAKE YOUR POSITION!

Creating space for your voice is the opening of new opportunities for your life. Before you proceed to the next section of the book, you must take your position:

1. **Stand in Your Authentic Voice** – You were not created to just occupy space in the world. You were created to make space. That means you can no longer hoard "stuff" that covers up your authentic voice. You can no longer let others dump on your authentic voice. You cannot continue to suffer in traumatic silence and languish in Post Traumatic Silence Disorder (PTSD). You must disrupt the silence and recover your authentic voice. Your journey to voice freedom will be futile without your authenticity. This is not an option. It is a must! You've got this!

2. **Harness Your Power** – You are more powerful than you have given yourself credit for being. It is just that your power has been buried under clutter. Here is where you

unbury it. No one else can have it! No one else deserves it! No one else can take it! Here is where you commit to never give it away again. You've got this!

3. **Master Your Influence** – There are others relying on you to create your space. When you do, it will give them permission to create their own. In essence, your journey is not just about you. There are others watching. They need your authentic voice to show up. It is literally light in the dark places in which they find themselves. Make your voice visible to them. They need you. You've got this!

MY VOICE COMMITMENT LETTER

Dear _____

Today, I commit to:

_____

_____

_____

_____

_____

_____

_____

_____

_____

Love,

_____

CHAPTER FOUR

Protecting Your Voice (Voice Security)

CHAPTER FOUR
Protecting Your Voice (Voice Security)

*Your authentic voice is private property. Don't allow others
to trespass.* ~Dr. K

Some of my darkest moments in time occurred as a consequence of what I spoke out of my mouth. In my excitement and zeal, I haphazardly entered into conversations with those who did not have my best interest in mind. I dialogued with those who only sought information for their own gain, ungodly motives, or selfish ambition. I entered into conversations with the purest intent to provide information, only to find that the recipients of what I provided were the least grateful, the most envious, and the ones that secretly hoped for my failure.

I entertained conversations with those I considered close to me, sharing what I perceived to be the purpose for my life, only to see the covert workings of their jealousy and competition. My good intentions became my source of hurt and left me spiraling in disappointment. But more importantly, these conversations weakened me and made me vulnerable to more of the same. Why? Because out of my wounds, I began a cycle of behavior to either try to prove something to the ones I never should have entertained.

Our unwise conversation can be the channel by which we give away our power. It is these conversations that get us into the most horrible trouble. When we speak, how we

speak, what we speak, and to whom we speak becomes the catalyst for a downward trajectory in our lives.

The "Thing" In My Gut

I was a giver by nature. I was also very trusting of those to whom I gave. Notice, I am speaking in the past tense. It is not that I no longer give or am no longer trusting, it is just that I had to learn to sprinkle it with wisdom. And, I learned this lesson the hard way.

Even as I write what I am about to share with you, I am still feeling that same "thing" in my gut I felt when I realized that a person I trusted with my thoughts, ideas, and work, ripped me off. I can recall the location, the space, and even the chair I was sitting in when I began sharing my vision for what I was passionate about.

She listened intently and with great interest. Taking notes feverishly, she asked question after question. I gave answer after answer. I remember thinking, "Oh my goodness! She is really into what I am saying. During our dialogue, she kept saying she had been thinking some similar things and that we should collaborate. I was all in!

Over time, I continued to share, pour out, and put it all on the table. However, I began to notice something...the sharing was only happening on my end. She wasn't sharing anything. Instead, I began seeing glimpses of what I had shared with her beginning to show up in the work she was putting out. I saw some of my ideas, my thoughts, and even the use of some of the same language.

In denial, my inner voice made excuses for her. It's not really what you think it is. She wouldn't do that. It's just your imagination. I rationalized and desperately tried to talk myself out of the "thing" in my gut. But, the reality is, it was exactly what I thought it was. What's worse, it was my fault. I had failed to guard my authentic voice. Without pause, I trusted her with my thoughts, ideas, and vision. I did not let down my guard. The truth is, I didn't know I needed one.

My initial response to her actions was hurt and disappointment. However, the more I thought about it, I found myself very angry with her. I lost respect for her and judged and labeled her in my head and heart. Every time I saw her, it triggered the thing in my gut. I relived the experience over and over again.

But the reality is, I was directing my energy toward the wrong source. She didn't steal anything from me. I left the door open. She didn't bombard her way in. I invited her in. She didn't overstep my boundaries, I never established any with her. She didn't threaten me. I felt threatened by her actions. She didn't hold me hostage. I became her hostage because I allowed actions to bind and gag me. Yes. She did what she did. However, I gave her the opportunity.

Protecting Your Property

I recently had a new state-of-the-art security system installed in my home. Equipped with video cameras, detectors, sensors, and monitoring, my home felt like it had everything except secret service. In addition to all the bells and whistles, there was an automated voice that told me everything happening in an around my home. For example, the system would alert me if someone was approaching the house, a door was opened, heat or fire was detected, and if the alarm was deactivated. I felt safe in the house and I felt that my valuables were safe when I was away.

I could lock my doors remotely from the app on my cell phone and I could speak to anyone standing on my doorstep from wherever I was. I had complete control of the system at all times. Having this kind of power was well worth the cost, so I didn't mind the monthly investment for the system.

The truth of the matter is, I don't know of anyone who would not want to protect what they own. Recognizing the value of what they have acquired, I believe they would go to extra lengths to keep their property safe from harm.

So, why is this not always the case with your authentic voice? Why is it that your most valuable possession is often left unguarded? It is because we are often more concerned about what we can give others and less concerned about what is being taken away from us in the process. In other words, in the process of giving, we are not aware of just how much we are losing. Because we are not aware, we give, and give, and give. Without boundaries and parameters, we give. Until that day, we wake up empty – with nothing left to give to anyone.

Have you ever been there? You know, feeling liked you've been robbed because you gave so much, it left you depleted? What's often very interesting about this place is that the ones who actually took from you can't seem to understand your emptiness. Instead, they keep coming back for more, waiting for you to give again.

Well, here is the truth. You taught them how to respond to you that way. It really is true. We teach others how to treat us, and the lesson you taught is that they could disregard you, but still get what you had to give. Why? You failed to protect your property.

Let's break this down. Because you did not position your authentic voice, you deactivated your alarm system. Therefore, you were not alert to the fact that something or someone was approaching you and would ultimately drain your spirit. You did not pay attention to the fact that you left the door open for them to walk right in. Because your internal alarm system was deactivated, you had no bells and no whistles. Because you left your authentic voice unprotected, you became a target and not a threat.

Voice Action: What comes to mind for you when you consider this notion of being a target and not a threat? Pause and really consider the implications of what that means for your life. *Tell yourself the truth about it...*

_____

_____

_____

_____

_____

_____

Reactivate Your System

Now that you recognize you have had a security breach, it's time to get your system activated. The breach occurred the moment you allowed something or someone to bypass your underlying security mechanism – your authentic voice. As a result, you allowed them to gain access to unauthorized parts of you. But, because your system was deactivated, you were unaware of the bypass.

From The Research

Revisiting experiences of physical and verbal abuse from a previous marriage, a research study participant associated her loss of voice with the power of another over her. Consequently, she expressed what she perceived as the insignificance of her voice. This silence belief ultimately led to self-muting and a loss of self-worth. As a result, the study participant admitted to her inability to hear and/or identify her own voice.

Overtime, this study participant lost sight of her value. The truth of the matter is, you will not protect what you don't value. You will not deny access to intruders and your authentic voice will be left open for attack. However, all is not lost. You simply need to reactivate your system. Let's begin...

Sensors, Motion, Cameras...Oh My!
Sensors

I have found that many of us fail to protect our authentic voice because we are not sensitive to what's going on around us. It's like the time I learned a few teenagers had been breaking into cars in a neighborhood close to mine. It never dawned on me that my car could ever be unsafe in my neighborhood. Call me naive, but I never considered it. I felt my neighborhood was a good safe neighborhood. I believed my neighbors were kind and they would never violate the property of other neighbors. But here is the reality, the neighbors were not the ones breaking in. The break-ins were happening from others outside the neighborhood.

The point is, there are those who are close to us and we have established a level of trust with them. Because we trust them, we often leave ourselves open to everyone. But the truth is, we simply cannot trust everyone. I don't want to sound cynical here. I simply want to point you toward an increased sensitivity to your surroundings. I want you to be sensitive to who you grant easy access to your authentic voice. I want you to readily detect the motion of an intruder in your life. More specifically, I want you to detect when someone is in your life that poses a threat to your well-being.

Motion

In order to do this, you've got to watch the movement of people in every area of your life. Again, this is not about being paranoid. It is about being protective. One of the most difficult lessons I learned came as a result of inviting people into my life and sharing far more than I ever should have. Because I had a false sense of safety, I let them in on happenings in my life they never should have had access to. I shared and trusted, shared and trusted, and shared and trusted. When what I shared was ultimately mishandled, I still chalked it up to the person being untrustworthy. It took several rounds of experiencing the sting of mishandled information for me to realize that the other persons were not the real issue. The real issue was the fact that I was not aware of my own pattern.

You see, most thieves are able to be successful because they study the patterns of their victims in order to plan when to strike. I was so open with my patterns that I became an easy prey. I was predictable, and I was unguarded. I left myself wide open. So, how could I fully blame the thief for taking from me when the thief was there by invitation?

Again, this is not about removing vulnerability from your life. I believe there is great power in being vulnerable. This is about being alert as to how you allow movement in your space.

Just like when there is movement in a home where there is a security system and the system is armed, any motion inside the house will send a signal and trip the system to alert the owner that there is a threat in the home. You must arm your system so you are appropriately responsive to the signals when your system is tripped (triggered).

Cameras

One of the most useful aspects of my alarm system in my home is the video camera on the doorbell. Whenever motion is detected around my front door, I am sent a notification to my cell phone. At that point, I am able to access the video camera and to see the movement on the person on my doorstep. I can see when they arrive, and I can see what they are doing while they are there. I can choose to speak through the speaker in the system, or I can choose to just watch them. The best part is, I can determine if I am going to let them in or not.

Protecting your authentic voice will mean you monitor your doorstep. You watch the arrival of those who show up in your life. You watch how they come. You watch what they do when they get there. You determine if and how you want to speak to them. You determine if you will let them in or not.

Voice Action: There is no doubt in my mind that you can relate to this section of the book. How do I know? I know because in all the clients I've coached and the conversations I've had, I have not met a person who told me they have ALWAYS made the best choices about who to allow in their life. You may be the exception. If you are, please email me at Katrina@re-sourcesolutions.com. I want to see how we can get you in the Guinness Book of World Records. The truth of the matter is, we have all felt the impact of leaving our authentic voice unprotected. We have felt that... "I never should have let them in" moment. We have felt the regret, the hurt, the disappointment, and the like. So, since that part is established, I want to ask you, *how will you apply a new approach? In what areas will you increase your sensitivity? What patterns are you going to change? How will you monitor the movement of others in your life? What protective measure will you take?*

Heat, Fire & Carbon Monoxide … Oh My!

Heat

Another feature of the alarm system in my home is its ability to detect not only intruders on the outside, but to detect the threat of harm going on inside the home. For example, the system will alert me if the temperature in the home rises beyond what is safe. It will send a notification to my cell phone and sound an alarm.

Just like I coach clients in ways to harness their power and master their influence related to their silence, I also have many clients whom I coach related to managing the "heat of the moment" in their lives. These are the clients whose emotional temperature rises beyond what is safe. Can you relate? Let's explore the feeling a little more with a few examples. It's the feeling when you are so triggered by something someone says or does:

- You feel the heat rising from your toes
- You feel the heat when it reaches your belly and forms a knot
- You feel the knot move up to your throat and become a lump there

- You feel the pounding of the lump in your throat
- You feel your nostrils flare and your breaths speed up
- You feel your face tingle from the heat
- You feel...

The "heat of the moment" is a powerful thing. Our emotions are high, and we feel the "heat" in every fiber of our being. It is at this point where the heat we feel becomes the driver for what we do. Of course, the temptation is to respond. However, there is much to be considered before you do. Navigating the heat of the moment is critical to protecting your authentic voice, which is also your reputation. For this reason, it is imperative to get an emotional grip in the midst of the heat.

Now, I am certainly not suggesting this is an easy feat when everything on the inside of you is heated. Think about it. The times you've gotten heated in a situation and responded negatively in that moment, was the outcome what you'd hoped for? Or, did it leave you feeling the regret of what you said and did?

For most, the heat of the moment leads to the regret of the moment. It leads to words you wish you could take back and actions you wish you could undo. The heat of the moment is where relationships are damaged, hearts are broken, spirits are wounded, and authentic voice is sabotaged.

However, the heat of the moment can be the place where you win! It is where you pause long enough to remember everything we have covered in this book thus far – your authenticity, your confidence your visibility and your security. The heat of the moment is not worth you undoing what you are working hard to do – that is positioning your authentic voice for positive and powerful impact. The heat of the moment is your opportunity to win! However, in order to do it, you must step out the heat and stand in your ability to remain cool, especially when it's hot.

Voice Positioning Points for
THE HEAT OF THE MOMENT

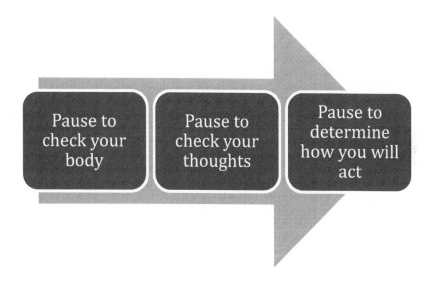

Voice Positioning Point One: Pause to Check Your Body

At the moment you are triggered, check-in with your body. Check the heat in your toes, the thing in your gut, the lump in your throat, the flare in your nostrils, and any other bodily response to the heat. Your body is your thermostat. It is able to sense the temperature and return it to the desired set-point. In other words, when your internal temperature begins to rise in the heat of the moment, you can adjust your body. This process begins with your thoughts.

Voice Positioning Point Two: Pause to Check Your Thoughts

Being triggered doesn't just set-off a burst of emotions. Being triggered also unleashes thoughts you would have never imagined you would be thinking. Like rapid fire, these thoughts ricochet off the walls of your brain, creating enough friction to raise the heat. However, this is the place where you pause long enough to dismiss the thoughts that will not serve you well. When you pause here, you are able to begin the conversations you need to have with yourself before you attempt to respond to others during the heat. This will allow you to consider your actions before you act.

Voice Positioning Point Three: Pause to Consider How You Will Act

"Watch your thoughts, they become words; watch your words, they become actions; watch your actions, they become habits; watch your habits, they become character; watch your character, for it becomes your destiny." This quote has been attributed to a number of people. However, I am sharing it as an illustration of the power of our thoughts and how they can direct our lives. I also want you to notice how often "watch" is mentioned in the quote. In the heat of the moment, it is critical to watch yourself! Pause long enough to be alert to what's happening on the inside of you so you can get clear about the most powerful way to act. In other words, watch your voice! The heat of the moment can make or break you. It's always your choice.

Fire

One of the most important features of an alarm system in a home is its ability to detect fire. Beyond heat detection, when the system detects fire, it not only sends a notification and sounds an alarm; it also contacts the fire department and dispatches them to the home.

Just as you have experienced the heat of the moment, there is no doubt you have also found yourself in what feels like a walk through fire. Whether in relationships, at work, or in other areas of your life, you've had to navigate burning issues and situations. This is a hard place, a challenging place, and the place that can certainly cause you to step away from your authentic voice.

When I reflect on my times in the fire, I can honestly say, protecting my authentic voice was the last thing on my mind. Instead, my focus was on freeing myself from what was burning. All I could think about was what I could do to get out of the fire. I analyzed and strategized ways to leave the issue or situation. It seemed my exit strategy was all I could think about. Let's be real, who wants to remain in a fire?

While I was deliberating ways to get out, I never recognized the power I had to fight the fire. I was so busy trying to escape it I did not own the power I had to stand up to it. Like the alarm system in the house, when fire is detected it dispatches fire fighters. Likewise, when things are on fire in your life, you must dispatch your own firefighter, your authentic voice, to fight the fire.

This means instead of running away, you confront the fire so it does not have the opportunity to destroy the house. In other words, you position your authentic voice in a way that allows you to save what is valuable to you (your authenticity, your confidence, and your space) instead of abandoning it and allowing it to burn.

Voice Positioning Points for
NAVIGATING THE FIRE

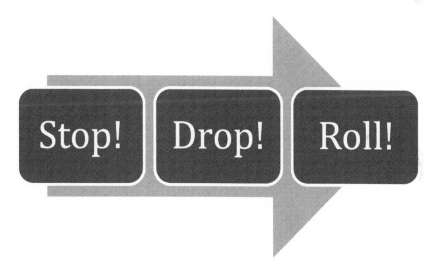

Voice Positioning Point One: Stop!

The moment you realize you are in the midst of a fire, this is the time you stop. You cease movement, so you don't fan the flames. This means be still. I know this sounds strange. However, it is when you are willing to be still that you can get clarity regarding what you should do in a crisis.

Voice Positioning Point Two: Drop!

This is the point at which you drop low to the ground. For me, this is the place of prayer. This is the place where I recognize I will not survive the fire without spiritual guidance. It is at this place where I find the wisdom and strength to know how to extinguish the flames.

Voice Positioning Point Three: Roll!

This is the place where you focus on depriving the fire of oxygen. This means you don't give the fire life. In essence, you become intentional not to fuel the fire through a misalignment of your authentic voice. Instead, you position your voice to gain control of the flames.

Carbon Monoxide

The real value of the alarm system is the fact that it is able to detect carbon monoxide. This feature is overwhelmingly significant because it is sensitive to the presence of a deadly gas that cannot be seen or heard. Carbon monoxide is a colorless and odorless gas and is literally a silent killer.

Protecting your authentic voice will often mean you must protect it from things working against you that cannot be seen or heard. For instance, one of my clients shared with me the devastation she felt when she learned someone very close to her had betrayed her trust. On a number of occasions, the client kept saying, "What makes this so hard is the fact that I never saw it coming."

Think about those times in your life when it seemed as if something was able to slip in and you were not aware until you felt the pain of something it killed. For my client, trust died. You may have experienced the death of other things – joy, peace, faith, or love.

You see, carbon monoxide poisoning usually occurs from breathing in too much carbon monoxide to the degree it becomes harmful over time. Therefore, there are warning signs that precede poisoning – confusion, blurred vision, weakness, and loss of consciousness. But if you are asleep, what you are breathing in will kill you.

My question to you is, have you been sleeping in the presence of poison? Have you gotten so comfortable in your surroundings that you don't recognize it is no longer safe to be there? Have your senses become so dull to your authentic voice that you are allowing it to die a slow death? If this is you … WAKE UP!

As you read these words, let this be your alarm. You cannot continue to exist in a contaminated environment and expect to remain alive. No! A toxic person will kill something in you! A toxic environment will kill something in you!

When you consider how to position your authentic voice in the presence of danger you cannot see, the first thing to do is watch what you're breathing in. You will not always know when something or someone poisonous enters your presence. However, at the moment you begin to experience adverse symptoms, you must get out of there and get to a place where you can breathe fresh air again.

Voice Action: Consider your surroundings and do a deep assessment. *Who or what could possibly be at the core of confusion in your life? Who or what may be causing your vision for your life to become blurry? Who or what is robbing you of your energy and making you weak? Who or what is redirecting your attention in such a way that it causes you to lose consciousness of your authentic voice and truth?*

_____

_____

_____

_____

_____

_____

"NO!"

My sister and I took a women's self-defense class. Initially, our thought was it would be great sister-time and loads of fun. Now, while all of that was true, the experience was powerful. Our time was spent learning special techniques to leverage our power to defend ourselves against anyone whose intention was to harm us.

The most powerful part of what we learned was that with every move, we were to yell, "NO!" Imagine a room filled with women yelling

"NO" as we went through the motions of defending ourselves. It was awesome! We left the class more knowledgeable, aware of our strength, and fully confident in our ability to protect ourselves if we were ever placed in a situation where we needed to do it.

But, I also left with a big, "What if" in my mind and heart. What if we were able to learn to protect our authentic voice? What if we learned the powerful use of, NO?! What if we leveraged the strength of our authentic voice to position it in a way that when there was an intention to cause us harm, we would not be defeated? What if we were willing to fight to protect it? What if…

Protecting Your Voice Will Cost You Something

Before the security system was installed in my home, a representative from the company walked me through the costs associated with the system. There was a cost for the sensors, the detectors, the cameras, and the monitoring. However, because of my intention to protect my property, I was willing to make the investment.

My Hope For You…

I am certain by now you have recognized the tremendous value of your authentic voice. My hope for you is that you are willing to make the sacrifice to protect it. This means you are willing to:

- Stay alert to your surroundings
- Separate yourself from situations that are not healthy for you to remain
- Let go of what is toxic
- Wake up…so you can live

Protecting your authentic voice will cost you something. My hope is that you will commit to making the investment. Your return will be priceless!

TAKE YOUR POSITION!

Protecting your voice is the key to your voice security. Before you proceed to the next section of the book, you must take your position:

1. **Stand in Your Authentic Voice** – You have an invaluable possession. You must protect it at all costs. You've got this!
2. **Harness Your Power** – You have an internal security system. It is time for you to activate or reactivate it. You've got this!
3. **Master Your Influence** – When you protect your voice, you also protect those around you from the misalignment of it. You've got this!

MY VOICE COMMITMENT LETTER

Dear _____

Today, I commit to:

_____

_____

_____

_____

_____

_____

_____

_____

_____

Love,

_____

CHAPTER FIVE

Nurturing Your Voice (Voice Care)

CHAPTER FIVE
Nurturing Your Voice (Voice Care)

If you don't take care of your voice, you cannot be surprised when it goes away. ~Dr. K

I facilitated a training on interpersonal awareness. At the end, I asked each participant to write a statement of commitment related to what they intended to do differently going forward. Many of the participants shared powerful intentions related to how they would connect with others more, how they would invite the stories of others, and how they would have more meaningful conversations.

However, one participant stood, and as she lifted her paper to read, she burst into tears. After several seconds of being unable to speak, she said, "I told myself I wasn't going to cry. But, I am crying because I've been silent, and I've been holding it all inside. I've been here for over a decade and I just remain in my cubical and do my work. Yeah, I talk, and I say a lot of things. But, I am still silent because I am not saying the things I need to say. I've put a wall up and it's really affected me over the years. Keeping my real voice inside has hurt me in a lot of ways. My commitment will be to take the wall down and let my voice out."

After she sat down, she cried until the end of the training. For her, this was truly and opening of the floodgates and allowing her authentic voice to pour out. The most phenomenal part is, by the time she left the session; everything about her was different. Her countenance, her demeanor, and her presence had shifted, all because she decided to commit to releasing her voice and caring for it in a new way.

Voice-Care

I share this experience with you because it is a powerful example of what happens to us when we don't practice voice-care. In other words, when we don't prioritize our authentic voice and nurture it as a core component of our well-being, we sabotage its health and we suffer the consequences in our mind, our body, and our spirit.

From The Research

A research study participant displayed signs of having resigned from her organization, although she showed up for work every day. Specifically, resignation represented the withdrawal from various aspects of the work and/or within the workplace. While still showing up for work on a daily basis, she described experiences and feelings associated with being present in body but having resigned mentally and emotionally. In response to power systems of hierarchal leadership, structures, governance, and/or operations, she discussed unique feelings associated with the ways in which she had left the organization without actually leaving. Furthermore, she shared how her state of being had affected every area of her life, mainly her physical health.

If you search, you can find article after article, book after book, tip after tip, and quote after quote on the importance of self-care. Although television, radio and social media are filled with ideas and products targeted toward caring for yourself, it is possible to practice self-care and still miss the nurture and care your authentic voice needs.

In fact, many of my clients have shared with me that they plan "me time" on a regular basis. This is the time they set aside for things like, spa days, time with friends, stay-cations, and vacations. The focus of their "me time" is generally rest and relaxation.

However, I have never heard any of my clients, or anyone else for that matter, say to me, "I really need some 'me time' so I can nurture and care for my authentic voice."

I know you may be thinking voice-care can happen in the process of self-care. However, I want to show you the difference. Self-care typically focuses on *doing* things for yourself, that contribute to your health and well-being.

Voice-care, on the other hand, focuses on a way of *being* that allows you to harness your power and master your influence. In essence, the differences exist in *doing* vs. *being*. This chapter will focus on nurturing your authentic voice, not solely by what you do, but by what you make the choice to *be*. Okay? Let's go!

Be Quiet and Still

As you know, the premise for this book emerged from my research on the phenomenon of organizational silence. So, much of the book's content has focused on harnessing your power and mastering your influence related to emerging out of silence that is detrimental to your well-being and living your authentic voice. However, it is at this point in the process where we talk about the silence as a way to nurture your voice.

You see, sometimes we underestimate the power of silence as a communication strategy. Those instances when everything in you is screaming to respond, when you know your blood pressure would go down a few notches if you could just say something, or when you have already reasoned that you will repent after it's all over, are the best times to practice silence.

This is where you take a "P.P. Break" (Personal Pause) and you step back and process before you respond (we discussed this in chapter 4). Your process may include self-talk, breathing, prayer, counting, or all of that. The point is to consider the best outcome. This is your opportunity to prevent regret. Most importantly, it is here where you guard your reputation and consider the consequence before it becomes a consequence. This is the point at which your silence (if even for a moment) becomes golden.

From The Research

A research study participant shared deeply about her perceptions and experiences of silence. Her responses demonstrated feelings related to a holistic approach to choosing silence or voice. She expounded, "I think that sometimes silence gets a bad rap. I don't think silence is always a bad thing. I think sometimes it's good to be still and just listen.

In my sessions with my clients, I remind them to stay out of their "back pockets"! Symbolically, there is something in your right back pocket and something in your left. These two things you don't want to pull out. In your right pocket is the phrase, "Frist of all…" and in your left pocket is the phrase, "What you are not going to do is…". If you find yourself beginning your sentence with either of these phrases, what comes next is probably not going to be good. So stay out of your pockets so you can take care of your authentic voice.

I cannot assure you that being quiet in the moment will feel good. But keeping your power is not about a feeling, it's about holding on to your strength, keeping your dignity, and making the right choices concerning how to position your voice.

Too Much Talk

The other part of being quiet and still is simply not talking so much. In other words, not talking just for the sake of talking. A part of nurturing your authentic voice is being thoughtful about when to position it. Everything does not require your input or opinion.

Think about the times you have been in the presence of a person and while they were talking, all you could think about was how you wished they would just be quiet. Well, don't be that person that others are wishing the same thing about. Be quiet and still long enough to determine your best voice contribution in any given situation.

Some believe that an effective use of voice is the bullhorn approach – loud and aggressive. While there may be a place and time for that approach, it doesn't serve you well for that to be the approach you use at all times. Ask yourself, would you want some loud aggressive voice in your ear at all times? I am sure your answer is, no. Therefore, others will appreciate you not being the loud aggressive voice in theirs.

From The Research
Certain of the power of her voice, a research study participant approached the balance between silence and voice behaviors with a sense of control. Recognizing her ability to determine when and how she would position her voice, she was able to compartmentalize the feelings of frustration, pain, anxiety, and anger connected to perpetual silence in the organization. With the desire for the health of the organization and for her own sense of well-being, she was driven by needing to make the choice to position her authentic voice in a way that would be a positive influence on others.

Being quiet and still will require you to assess your *paraverbal communication*, that is, your tone, pitch, and pacing of your voice. It will require you to check your style and consider your approach. You cannot [not] communicate, because everything is a message. The goal in nurturing your authentic voice is to ensure you care for it in a way that allows you to position it positively and powerfully. Even when you're passionate about what you want to communicate, you must be aware and strategic in how you do it.

Be Aware and Strategic

One of my corporate clients called me in to provide executive coaching for a leader who was challenged in her communication style. When I met with her supervisors, they gave me examples of her behavior when others were speaking in meetings and when others were attempting to provide feedback to her. They explained that she rolled her eyes. She made deep sighs. She shook her head in a "no" motion. She folded her arms and shifted in her seat.

Not knowing what her supervisors had shared with me, in my initial session with her, we discussed her perceptions of her communication. She shared with me that she believed she was a very good communicator. I asked her to give me a few examples of how she communicates in meetings. She shared, "For the most part, I'm quiet. I usually don't say anything because much of what is being discussed I don't agree with. So rather than voice my frustration, I'm just quiet." I said, "Okay. Show me how you're quiet when you're frustrated. What does that look like?" In her demonstration, she did exactly what her supervisors said she was doing.

The part of this scenario that is most interesting is that she readily reenacted her behavior and didn't see the problem with it. When I pointed out what I observed, it was as if I was talking about someone she had never met before. She was so unaware of herself until when I mirrored back her actions. They had been unrecognizable to her.

From The Research

A research study participant's shared perceptions and experiences of silence in the organizations where she worked highlighted ways in which the power interwoven into systems served to fuel organizational dynamics that led to her silence. With great confidence and strength of voice prior to coming to the organization, over time she was met with systemic realities in leadership, structure, and expectations that ultimately

---

served to mute her voice and generated feelings of "pulling back" – leading to communicating her frustration in silence.

Being aware of yourself at all times is critically important to nurturing and caring for your voice. Not only is it necessary to be aware, it is also important to be strategic in how you are positioning your authentic voice.

You will always have nonverbal communication. The strategy is to be intentional regarding your nonverbal communication. This will require you to be mindful of yourself and become an excellent observer of your own processes.

Oftentimes it is easier to point our finger at others as the reason for our actions, but the truth of the matter is, no one can make you do anything. It is always your choice. For this reason, powerful voice positioning is predicated on what you choose.

Therefore, being strategic will require you to listen to the language of your body before anyone has an opportunity to hear that language (note: you do know body language is loud, right?). That means you must be mindful of how your body typically responds to triggers so that you can counteract the triggers and make adjustments with the most appropriate language at any given moment.

Being aware and strategic will also require you to suspend your immediate judgment of others until you have given yourself enough time to process and to obtain enough information to give an informed response. In other words, you must keep your mind and your heart clear of clutter so when you respond, you don't give out garbage. This will give you an opportunity to be discerning and disregarding.

Be Discerning and Disregarding

When you are able to discern a situation, you can disregard the parts that will rob you of your energy and sabotage your authentic voice. It is here where you are able to determine what is valuable to you so you don't become discombobulated by what is not.

Allow me to break this down a bit more. Let's consider relationships. There are some people in our lives that bring with them a number of dynamics and characteristics. In much of what they bring, you may find tremendous value. However, there are other parts, that perhaps, as my five-year-old niece would say, "gets on your last nerves." In these instances, you maintain the relationship because you have learned to take the parts that work and leave the other parts alone. At least, I hope you have learned that lesson.

The way you distinguish between the good parts and the parts that leave much to be desired, is through your ability to determine what your genuine needs are. When you are clear about what you need, you also become clearer about the things you don't. This level of clarity allows you to manage your expectations of yourself and your expectations of others. This will also be your guide related to how much you can and should give back, keeping in mind, everyone does not have the same capacity you do. Therefore, you must treat each relationship according to its capacity to sustain what you have to offer it and what you will receive from it.

Keep in mind, disregarding is not about disregarding a person. You don't get to throw people away. This is about disregarding the actions that do not deserve your attention or energy. Additionally, this does not mean you don't address actions that are misaligned with what you value. It means that once it is addressed, you "bless and release" so you can continue to move forward. Remember, the goal is to nurture and care for your authentic voice. Therefore, you must know that your voice is a terrible thing to waste.

Voice Action: At this point in the chapter you have learned the critical necessity of "Being" related to nurturing and caring for your authentic voice. We have covered the value in being quiet and still, aware and strategic, and discerning and disregarding. *When you consider these core components as foundational for how you position your voice in order to harness*

> *your power and master your influence, what adjustments are you ready to make in these areas?*
>
> _____
>
> _____
>
> _____
>
> _____
>
> _____
>
> _____

Be Emotionally Sensitive and Socially Intelligent

There has been a lot of research on emotional intelligence. Daniel Goleman and other scholars have explored self-awareness, self-regulation, motivation, empathy, and social skill as core components needed to be emotionally intelligent. Most of the research has focused on emotional intelligence as a leadership competency and the need for emotional dexterity for effective leadership.

While I have a great appreciation for the research, for the purpose of positioning your voice in a way that allows you to harness your power and master your influence, I want to take us beyond emotional intelligence to emotional sensitivity.

The premise for this reframing is an understanding that before we can be intelligent, we must be able to quickly detect a need to be intelligent. In other words, intelligence is an outcome. However, sensitivity is being highly aware of the stimuli (triggers) that cause us to respond. Therefore, being sensitive to our tendencies and patterns of our emotions will then help us to make intelligent choices regarding our response in spite of our emotions.

Nurturing and caring for your authentic voice will require you to pause long enough to listen to what your emotions are speaking to you. Once you have heard, you can determine your response, keeping in mind the response that is most appropriate may be in contrast to what you actually feel. Being emotionally sensitive allows you to align your emotional intelligence for the most powerful outcome.

From The Research

Managing feelings of intimidation related to speaking up, a research study participant became a contributor to organizational dialogue, even when the invitation was not extended to her to do so. Furthermore, in the face of feelings of frustration related to the impact of instances when she was silent, she was resilient as she recoiled from silence with feelings of resoluteness related to recapturing and sustaining her voice. With authenticity as the central component to her pursuit of voice, her voice commitment generated a feeling of personal and organizational responsibility for speaking up.

I also want to address the notion of social intelligence. The definition dates back to the 1920's and is described as, "the ability to act wisely in human relations." Much of what we have discussed thus far in this book is related to your ability to act wisely in human relations. In fact, positioning your authentic voice with power and influence is directly connected to your capacity to navigate interpersonal and intergroup interactions.

Beyond some of the ways we have already discussed related to human relations, because of technological advances, we have so many more opportunities to be unwise in how we relate to others. While technology has evolved in brilliant ways, it has also created tremendous barriers to human interaction. Living in virtual worlds, having a real connection with others is decreasing. The irony is, social media forums encourage us to have "friends" and "followers". With that being said, I want to specifically address social intelligence on social media.

Nurturing and caring for your authentic voice are imperative if you are engaged in social media activity. While many of the forums were created to foster connection, the downside is that this form of virtual communication can also facilitate disconnection, division, and disrespect... often all in the name of freedom of speech.

In addition to hurt feelings and ruined relationships, false realities can also be created through profiles, posts, and statuses. In fact, one of my coaching clients shared with me the despair she felt every time she scrolled through her Facebook timeline because she felt she was not measuring up in life in comparison to the lives of her "friends". She had to fight the temptation to create a virtual life that was not authentically hers.

It took every ounce of professionalism in me to maintain my composure and not to yell at the top of my lungs, "Girl! The 'reality' you see is often not the 'reality' that is lived. You can't compare your life to one that doesn't really exist!" Instead, I simply asked her powerful coaching questions that helped her arrive at that conclusion on her own [Note: I don't yell at my clients (smile)].

Listen, I want to remind you your voice is your message to the world. I have witnessed so many people sabotage their world-message because they were unwise in their social media messaging. Not being socially intelligent in these instances cost them greatly. Think about those we've watched lose their jobs, friends, and family because of their choice not to honor human relations. Think about the number of people who are misled by false realities because appearance has become more important than authenticity.

For many, social irresponsibility has become the norm. However, nurturing and caring for your authentic voice is required, no matter the forum. Social media should not become the substitute for human connection. It should not be the replacement for crucial conversation. Taking social responsibility is the catalyst for social intelligence. Your commitment to powerfully positioning your voice is directly linked to how you perceive and interact with humanity. The goal is to be intentional in being sensitive and intelligent in the process. This is the path to no regrets... the path to harnessing your power and mastering your influence.

Be Sorry... Not Sorry

Now that we have talked about emotional sensitivity and social intelligence, I want to encourage you to approach these necessary components unapologetically. As a matter of fact, I want to encourage you to approach everything we've discussed unapologetically. Why? This is essential to nurturing and caring for your authentic voice.

Far too often we feel the need to apologize when we choose our well-being over all else. You would think others would want you to be well. But, the truth of the matter is, for some, your brokenness works better for them. Not positioning your voice, harnessing your power, and mastering your influence, keeps you subject to the control of other people, places, and things.

From The Research

A study participant grew up in a family with six siblings and was the first in her family to graduate from college, earning a Bachelor's and Master's degree. She was also the first in her family to obtain a professional job/career. Because she was the first in her family to accomplish educational and professional goals that others in her family had not, she expressed her struggle with the perceptions her parents and siblings maintained regarding her success. Although accomplished, she still felt an awkward sense of shame for achieving what others had not. As she reflected on the tension she experienced with her family, she shared, "I always felt pressure to stay at the level of my siblings and my parents so that I didn't exceed and be someone who they looked upon as trying to be too much." While she was very proud of her many milestones, when she spoke of her successes in the context of family, she spoke apologetically.

In the Voice Positioning Leadership Program I developed, one of the modules focuses on removing "I'm sorry" from your vocabulary. In this context, I am referring to the definition of "sorry" as being in a poor or pitiful state or condition. Allow me to point out this definition denotes being poor or pitiful. Please hear me, "sorry" is a state or a condition, not an identity.

There is never a reason to say that you are anything that is actually contrary to your authentic voice identity. You are never lesser. You are never inferior. You are never unworthy. You are never not enough...never. Therefore, you never need to apologize for your authenticity. You only need to nurture and care for it.

Voice Action: We have covered the value in being emotionally sensitive, socially intelligent, and sorry...not sorry. *When you consider these core components as foundational for how you position your voice in order to harness your power and master your influence, what adjustments are you ready to make in these areas?*

TAKE YOUR POSITION!

Nurturing your voice is the foundation for your voice-care. Before you proceed to the next section of the book, you must take your position:

1. **Stand in Your Authentic Voice** – Nurturing and caring for your authentic voice is critical to your journey. However, it will require your willingness to take a stance for your own well-being, even when your decision may not be popular. There is no doubt your choice to care for your voice will mean you must step away from the people, places, and things that are a barrier to this process. It will not be easy but stand anyway. I can assure you that you will be strengthened along the way as you consistently choose you. You've got this!

2. **Harness Your Power** – Everything you need to nurture and care for your authentic voice is already on the inside of you. Now, it is time for you to tap into what you already have. Your power is in your ability to harness that power in the most challenging times. But, now you know how to *Be*. You've got this!

3. **Master Your Influence** – Nurturing and caring for your authentic voice will have a direct influence on others. It is here where you can model positively impactful voice care for those around you. In order to master your influence, you must be committed and consistent. You've done the work. Now, let others see what you're working with. You've got this!

My Hope For You...

You will have many opportunities to not nurture and care for your voice. However, when you find yourself there, I hope you remember me asking you this question, "What kind of life will you live if you lose your voice?" In other words, now that you know the power of your authentic voice and the critical importance of positioning it effectively, are you willing to live a life without it? If so, you really can stop reading at this point because nothing else I say will help you.

However, if you are seriously committed, my hope for you is that you will not allow anything to interfere with your nurturing and care for your voice. I hope you will protect it by any means necessary. It is my hope you will make it your priority and that you won't compromise it. I hope you will need it like the air you breathe, with the recognition that without it, something will die.

MY VOICE COMMITMENT LETTER

Dear _____

Today, I commit to:

_____

_____

_____

_____

_____

_____

_____

_____

_____

_____

Love,

_____

CHAPTER SIX

Celebrating Your Voice (Voice Victories)

CHAPTER SIX
Celebrating Your Voice (Voice Victories)

"With every voice victory comes another level of freedom!"
~Dr. K

Have your ever experienced a time when it felt like you were facing the battle of your life? Did you feel as though your enemies surrounded you and the barrage of attacks were unyielding? Did you think to yourself, "This is it! There is no way I can win in this situation?" I sure have! In fact, an experience such as this changed my life and relationship with God forever.

It was as if one day I went to sleep and the next day, all hell had broken loose in my life. The onslaught came in such a way (to use my grandmother's terminology) that "I didn't know if I was coming or going."

Naturally, or should I say instinctively, my first response was to retreat and run for cover. My next thought was to retaliate and fight back with all my might. Lastly, I thought, "I've got to get out of here...I need a one-way ticket to anywhere...just not here!"

I felt the agony of defeat from the blows from my enemies. I felt the emotional abandonment when friends walked away in the heat of the skirmish. I felt the weight of helplessness at not being able to stop the attacks. I felt the shame of my defenseless and fearful state of mind.

Frustrated, confused, broken, and torn, I was quickly moving toward a resolve to give up. I didn't see how this was going to end, and I had grown tired of looking. I was at the end of myself. The fight in me was gone. My hope was drying up. In addition, I felt like my faith was failing me. I felt complete and utter defeat. Have you ever been there?

From The Research

A research study participant articulated feelings of exasperation connected to her perceptions of being unrecognized, undervalued, and somewhat invisible as a woman and as a mid-level leader in her organization. As a result of the identified systemic dynamics, she spoke transparently about her feelings of disappointment and a sense of defeat related to the lack of access to leadership and therefore having no opportunity to speak up. Experiencing the void of being uninvited to voice her opinion, she underscored ways in which hierarchal structures in the organization served to perpetuate silence, especially the silence of women.

Again, can you relate to this place? Over the course of my coaching career, I have coached hundreds of people who came to me because they felt defeated in some area of their life. They were tired from what seemed to be a continuous barrage of issues, conflicts, and challenges coming at them. They wanted to know how to move from under the heaviness of the attacks and how to move forward.

What was most interesting about this level of defeat was that it was internal. However, externally, they were keeping it hidden behind a smile (remember we discussed this in chapter one). Having been in that same place, one of the first coaching questions I asked them was, "Where is your victory?"

I ask this question because the truth of the matter is, if we are not careful, we will allow feelings of defeat to consume us to the degree that we forget all about the areas in our lives where we are winning. We will change our heart song to, "Nobody Knows the Trouble I See" and we will convince ourselves that this place of defeat, "is what it is." But, while we have moments of defeat, that's not where our narrative stops.

Because I believe so strongly in the power of your authentic voice, I also believe in its ability to override defeat. This is not about dismissing and/or masking issues, conflicts, and challenges. It is about recognizing the power of your authentic voice to overcome and conquer. This is not about fluff or a pie-in-the-sky approach to ignoring hard places in your life. It is about being careful not to allow hard places to silence you.

I wholeheartedly believe that you can flip the narrative by learning to celebrate your wins to the degree that you tap into your strength to address your defeat.

Think about it this way. I love basketball. I especially enjoy NBA games and being in the arena when the teams play. It's always interesting how the home team's arena has a system to keep their team motivated. There is nonstop upbeat songs, chants, and cheers about winning being piped through the speakers. It's booming loud! Even if the home team is losing, what's coming through the speakers doesn't stop. In fact, the songs, chants, and cheers get more frequent and much louder!

Ask yourself, when I feel defeated, do I turn off my internal speakers? Do I turn off my ability to hear the songs of my heart, my own chants of self-affirmation, and my cheers of encouragement? I want you to seriously consider these questions and your answers. You may find that you feel defeated because you stop your own celebration when it feels like you're not winning. However, I wholeheartedly believe that in order to effectively position your authentic voice, you cannot stop your own party…no matter how you feel.

You have read up to this point. No doubt, you have done some work, and you have had some wins in positioning your voice. However, did you pause to celebrate your wins? I mean really celebrate! Here is the good news; you still have time.

Voice Victory Stories

I want to invite you to read the voice victories of some phenomenal women who were excited to share with me for this book. Written in their own voices, they share powerful insight into their lessons, challenges, and actions related to positioning their authentic voices. As you read their brief stories, I ask that you reflect on your own. The goal in sharing the voice victories of others is to help you get your party started. Defeat cannot remain when you replace it with celebration. Go ahead and get your pom-poms ready! V-I-C-T-O-R-Y... VICTORY! VICTORY! THAT'S OUR CRY!!!

To be Completely Honest...

At the beginning of 2018 I would have described myself as bold but hesitant, determined but exhausted, and as Alanis Morissette said in *Hand in My Pocket*, sane but overwhelmed. As a *relatively* young, full-time working mother, my mental and physical work capacity was at an adequate level of satisfaction. However, I often felt stagnant and knew I wasn't meeting my full potential personally and professionally. Fortunately, my leadership at work recognized my prospective talent and offered me the opportunity to receive coaching from Dr. K.

When Dr. K asked me to share a little about myself, I explained how I was working on balancing career and family while also maintaining my home and making time for the gym a few days a week. What I quickly learned from that first session is we sometimes act abnormal when we are trying to achieve what we perceive as normal (i.e. to be happy and productive my life must be balanced). We discussed if a balanced life is necessary, or even realistic, and why we pressure ourselves to try to achieve it. It's hard to be your true, authentic self when you're trying to fulfill some unfeasible role that you assume society expects of you. Through a series of one-on-one sessions with Dr. K, I was able to talk about my feelings, my fears, and my successes without fear of judgement and with honest guidance in return.

I rediscovered my personal character strengths of honesty and perseverance. I always knew I was an honest, hard-working person, but I also knew there were many times in my life where I was holding myself back. When speaking the truth might cause pain, or when barriers, whether real or perceived, blocked my path, I hesitated, allowing fight or flight to take over, forgetting who I really was. Through Dr. K's coaching, I learned effective skills on how to overcome these situations to truly be fulfilled and successful.

In my profession I advocate for nutrition and physical activity policy, systems, and environmental changes at the state level to make the healthy choice the easy choice for all South Carolinians. To achieve these changes, I work with partners, including key decision makers, who sometimes appear unreachable. I serve as a leader in this capacity by facilitating, coordinating, and participating in various committees and coalitions. It takes focus, strong-will, and poise to lead a group of individuals, especially when challenges are faced, and difficult decisions need to be made.

To build on these facilitation skills, Dr. K tasked me with creating powerful communication by positioning my voice with my strength of honesty as a foundation. Whether in-person, on the phone, or through email, I stopped hesitating and became direct - saying what needed to be said or asking what needed to be asked but with a manner that wouldn't offend or be a detriment to the conversation. I began to notice partners who were silent before were now responding. Partners who were vague before were now more focused. Partners who seemed unreachable before were now making themselves available. All of their responses became more positive and honest, contributing to the overall group effort.

My ability to have an honest, possibly even painful, conversation was put to the test when I needed to discuss my concerns about the future of my career with my supervisor. In the world of public health, grants fund most, if not all, of the work we do. I recently received some disappointing news that a grant application I assisted with writing to sustain my current position wasn't funded. I was exhausted from putting so much time and energy into something that now felt as if it were all for nothing. I was defeated thinking that all of my efforts, all of my successes, and all of the work from the past five years would disappear.

Even though it put my stomach in knots, I shared these fears with my supervisor. I also shared my thoughts about moving to another agency if that's what I needed to do, even though it wasn't what I wanted to do. My supervisor, also an honest and direct person, reciprocated my directness which lead to a positive and powerful conversation. After only a few minutes into our discussion the knots in my stomach were gone, I could breathe easier, and I knew I had a leader who would advocate on my behalf to ensure my skills and expertise would continue to be applied and developed.

In order to grow I had to take risks. In order to take risks, I had to be my authentic self. In order to be my authentic self I had to recognize my strengths as an honest, persistent person. In order to be an honest, persistent person I had to grow. I've come full circle in the past six months, and I'm looking forward to where this journey of self-discovery will take me next.

Erica Ayers is a School Health Professional

Reflections on Internal Earthquakes

When I signed up for Dr. K's Voice Positioning System Leadership Program through the Junior League of Columbia, I did not foresee the impact it would have in detangling the deeper threads of my soul. I already considered myself confident and have held leadership positions amongst people 10+ years my senior throughout life so I wasn't aware how much space for growth I had within. This course has given me the inner tools to position my Voice in useful ways while consistently bringing my best assets to the forefront. I could spend all day writing on the earthquakes I've felt internally but will focus on two major core shifts in my day-to-day life.

The first is that I now act intentionally and consistently on all social fronts. I realized during the lectures that I often reign in my Voice and temper my normal personality in front of certain groups fearing it may be harshly judged or not accepted. Never mind that many terrific people do love and appreciate that same quirky personality when it is present! And the second breakthrough was digging through all the garbage I hoarded mentally and ultimately sending those thoughts to the dump where they belong; garbage such as past failures, unfulfilled goals, and lost relationships; garbage that I felt was on total display for the entire world to sift through at will, when in reality, nobody is allowed in the house of my soul unless I invite them. And now that I've cleared it out, the air is much sweeter.

During our fifth class, we did an exercise where we had to write a letter to ourselves. A statement of forgiveness and empowerment showing how we wish to move forward in life. I feel this letter, written to myself that night, reflects well the power this course has to completely transform the inner lives of women:

"Dear Lisa,

You will grasp your space in society and not revel in yesterday's failures. You will not criticize yesterday's tough choices with today's hindsight as those choices were made with the best resources available to you at the time.

There is no more assumed knowledge of totality when other people meet you. They do not care about your failures—they care how you treat theirs. You will embrace your life story, sign off on it, and leave messy chapters behind.

You will allow yourself compassion, kindness and gentleness. The same amount that you are known for showing others. You will be your own friend. You will forgive yourself, understanding the life you have built is a great one for the reality you were born into.

You will not compare your place in society to those around you. You will focus on your own goals and do your best. Not their best. You will continue to self-improve as you are driven, but with the knowledge that you are already enough just as you are now, from here on out, and forever more."

Lisa Cole is a mama and freelance writer.

My Voice Victory Take-Away:

_____

_____

_____

_____

_____

_____

The Power of a Silent Voice

I have unfortunately suffered too many times from a loss of my voice. Voice loss was clear to me in those moments based on my inability to be heard but also for my voice to be valued. I wish I could tell you it happened once or twice before I figured out what to do but it didn't. It continued to happen repeatedly in my life until silence became my default setting to uncomfortably frustrating situations. My silence became my safety. It kept me from forcing others to value my voice and my ideas. It hid me from opportunities I felt unqualified or deserving of in my life. It kept me safely in my seat from rocking the boat. I stayed in the box with everyone else daring to never peek out over the top into the place no one ventured. Oftentimes my voice was either foreign to those who had never heard it or too loud and aggressive to those who didn't want to hear it in the first place. Usually a voice in opposition no matter how sweet still requires a defense so to avoid misinterpretation, I safely stayed quiet.

I realized my voice loss was beginning to become more enduring than I desired. My safety was no longer working, and I was being mistreated now even in my silence. Somehow, my temporary treatment was becoming a long-term regimen to a situation never intended to be permanent. After weeks of spiritual devotion and personal development, I started an intentional focus on getting my voice back. I began daily morning and evening affirmations to myself. I wanted to hear Gods thoughts and promises for me flow from my lips, in my voice to guide me. My voice was important from what I said down to the texture and tone. The words of my voice guide what I think and where I focus daily transferring into what I ultimately choose to do. It is a voice of authority and intention for which I am responsible.

Then, one day, someone acknowledged their mistreatment of me; a mistreatment I never used my voice to acknowledge but manifested feelings of frustration and defeat resulting in a physical illness. I simply listened to the individual outline detailed events and the decisions to behave the way they had towards me. Once they were done, it was my turn. I could have used my power to retaliate, be angry, or offer my acceptance of the disclosure and go through an immediate healing process. I did none of the above. I chose to preserve my voice, reserve my power and energy at the moment to take care of me. My next steps were important and came from the discovery of my own voice power. Right there in the moment and conversation, I acknowledged what the individual said had been heard. I acknowledged the courage, strength, and professionalism it required, and we cordially ended the conversation. However, my process had just begun as I was able to identify the importance my voice had in the conversation.

The person did not ask for an apology. I don't know if one was wanted, needed or even expected. The person did not ask what I did or did not know about their actions and the role they played in private matters. The person did not ask me to share what I was feeling about what was said. So, my power was to silence my voice. I learned there was not a need to offer a response for every apology received, an incident of discomfort, or offensive action taken towards you. I reserve the right to be silent if I so choose. I use my voice deliberately. I control my responses because my voice and even my silence are valuable.

Dr. K has encouraged me to have these self-reflective moments regarding not just the voices around me but the voice I have before it ever makes a sound outside my being. I want my voice to be life-sustaining, not life-preserving. I have the power to choose when I turn my voice off and on, but I must never lose it again.

Naomi Washington is a social worker, author, speaker, and mentor

---

My Voice Victory Take-Away:

_____

_____

_____

_____

_____

_____

Be Authentic, Not Strategic!

Most of us were taught in the beginning of our careers that when interviewing you must make sure to 'tell them what they want to hear'. While that's true up to a point, many of us got so good at it that our true, authentic selves were completely masked - to the point it became a detriment to ourselves personally and professionally. We became unfulfilled and frustrated on our jobs. Employers wondered how the person they interviewed could be so different from the one that showed up daily.

While I've always been authentic personally, I found myself in that situation professionally more than once. I decided I had enough! In comes Dr. K, who encouraged me to use my authentic voice in my professional space where doing so as a woman and particularly as a Black woman is not always affirmed or received well. I took her advice and made up my mind to do so!

With my newfound confidence of fully owning my voice professionally I just knew this was going to be easy. It wasn't! I went into interviews speaking in my authentic voice and ultimately didn't get any of those jobs. I was like Wait...What? My faith was tested, and my authentic voice took a beating!

...But I'm here to say that when the right opportunity came about, my authentic voice and experience was EXACTLY what they wanted and needed. I spoke from my experience and my perspective. The process was smooth. I got the job that's right for me and the organization is getting the employee they feel they need...they'll be no surprises on either side. So, ladies owning your voice is essential...letting God stay in control, finding others who own their authentic selves to support you (I encountered plenty of 'phony superficial folks', 'fakers', and 'posers'...so beware) and understand it's a process. When the timing is right, it will all come together easily!

Thanks Dr. K,_for being a sistah-friend and being a blessing to others! You are the real deal!

Veronica Hemmingway is a community leader and philanthropist.

My Voice Victory Take-Away:

_____

_____

_____

_____

_____

PIECES, A Soulful Journey with Alopecia

I will never forget this statement, "Ms. Harris, I'm sorry to inform you that you have A-L-O-P-E-C-I-A!" Those were the words of my doctor as I sat in his office wondering why I had a bald spot on the crown of my head. Every word after that sounded like the school teacher on Charlie Brown because I was stuck at ALOPECIA. My emotions went spiraling out of control as I tried to understand what this meant. Questions like: How can this happen? Is there a cure? Why me? For days I asked God why did this have to happen to me, I remember saying to Him, really God? My hair? Why not something else? Something others could not see.

As an African American woman, my hair was my crowning glory and to have that negatively affected was devastating. Society places such a stigma on women who experience hair loss. The initial reaction to seeing a woman who is bald is to think she has some terminal illness. If not that, she is cast in the role of being less feminine. At the time of my diagnosis in 2007, I don't recall seeing or hearing much about women being celebrated, accepted, or applauded for exercising her right to choose baldness as her hair appearance. Now, there are some instances, such as mine where there is not much choice in whether we lose our hair, however, I still had a choice as to how I handled it.

I initially went to see a Dermatologist and underwent weekly injections in my scalp in hopes of hair restoration. I also went natural, per doctor's orders, because my hair follicles could not take any more chemicals. This process went on for months before I heard the next set of devastating words, "Ms. Harris, there is no cure and your hair will not grow back." I remember leaving the office that day feeling like I was in a bad dream and praying to wake up at any moment. Unfortunately, each day I woke up this issue was staring at me in the mirror. So, I decided to go on a journey with my hair or what was left of it and try to embrace the hand I had been dealt.

I spent the next 10 years wearing weaves, braids, wigs, and finally locs. I met a fabulous stylist that really took little and worked wonders. My self-esteem and self-worth were restored. I felt like a woman again, bold, beautiful and sexy and so all was right with the world. This lasted for a while but there was always the fear of others finding out and my secret being exposed.

See, I equated beauty to how my hair looked, heck, I equated it to having hair and the mere thought of that changing kept me bound like a prisoner. I would not share my condition with anyone outside of my family, close friends, and my stylist. I had no intent or concern for helping other women break free because I was captive myself. I did not see my situation as a blessing but in fact a curse. I didn't see how God could use this as a means of setting other women free because through my lenses all I saw was shame and embarrassment.

This year, my journey took a turn, and I went down the road of self-discovery. I decided this year that I wanted to put on my own oxygen mask before trying to help others. I began to put in the work that allowed me to journey towards healing inside and out. What I discovered about myself was that I was hiding. Hiding the beauty I was blessed with because I valued societal opinions over God spoken facts, I am fearfully and wonderfully made. His word did not say with hair or without. When faced with this revelation, I decided to allow my journey to take me to a place of bravery and let go of the things I used to hide my imperfection.

Much to my surprise, it was a very liberating experience filled with healing, grace, support, and love. I can truly say that I am freer as a bald woman than I ever was with the fiercest hairdo. Cutting and shaving my hair was a rite of passage into emotional wellness, spiritual maturity and overall wholeness.

I am proud to be a bald woman who is a voice for women who have not had the courage to be vulnerable in this area yet. Now, I use my baldness to educate others and my conversation starter is a simple phrase, "I'm bald and I don't have Cancer."

Alicia P. Harris is a therapist, advocate and motivational speaker.
Note: Alopecia is the partial or complete absence of hair from areas of the body where it normally grows. It affects approximately 6.8 million people in the United States and 147 million worldwide. www.naaf.org

My Voice Victory Take-Away:

_____

_____

_____

_____

_____

Afraid of Tears No More

I had a situation that I needed to use my voice, but due to emotions and holding back tears, my voice was quivering. I reached out and asked Dr. K how to you use your voice when it is quivering. The voice lesson she gave me was that your voice is not just words; your voice is your entire self. That my tears are a part of my voice, and that it is ok to cry. She helped me discover that my tears were my 'PP' (personal pause). By personal pause, I mean my tears are an extension of my voice, which allows me to 'pause' so I may collect myself. That personal pause allows my mind to calm and focus to amplify my voice.

My feeling of empowerment, the action plan we discussed, and my voice being amplified that day allowed me to face and resolve that situation instead of my normal withdrawing. My voice truly freed me that day, and I felt amazing by the end of the day.

She really showed me the power of my voice that day and I am so appreciative.

The knowledge you impart is so much more valuable than I think anyone actually understands until you try it. I did not fully understand until I saw it for myself; thank you very much Dr. K, for breaking away a piece of the shell that I usually hide under when it comes to conflict.

Salena Page-Black works in information technology
and is a mom, wife, and Animal Lover.

My Voice Victory Take-Away:

_____

_____

_____

_____

_____

My Voice is a Tool of Self-Advocacy

I recently read a quote that said, "Some view collaboration as the first step to their organization's elimination. When you have a "turfism" mindset, collaboration is a threat".

As a social entrepreneur in the non-profit field, this quote speaks truth to a recent experience that I had. An experience that was once filled with excitement that later turned to disappointment and pain. In my transparency, working through this experience has taken quite some time, and as I recently shared my experience in a public space, I could still feel the residue of hurt but also bitterness still there that I had to work thru.

However, I am also yet grateful because I realized that my voice had been impacted in several ways from this experience. The most powerful revelation for me was not only recognizing the importance of my voice but the value of my voice! For it can either create spaces for growth, hindrances, or doors to remain shut.

I realized that I can never expect others to value my voice if I first don't recognize and walk in it as the vessel of my own voice! So from this experience I am now committed to safely securing my voice and ensuring that it is given its worth and not taken advantage of.

Ashley Thomas is an executive director, academic success coach, and a blog contributor.

My Voice Victory Take-Away:

_____

_____

_____

_____

_____

_____

Hear Me ROAR!

I am a woman who was always known for being outgoing, enthusiastic, and positive; who always had a smile on her face. I had hit a huge hurdle in my life that had changed me, and to many, lessened me. I was verbally and emotionally abused by a work-partner for some time, and nothing was done about it. After diagnosed with severe PTSD, and beginning the road to recovery, a wonderful opportunity came into my life. I met an awesome stellar woman that made me see that there was light at the end of the tunnel, and it wasn't the end at all, but the beginning.

I have learned so much of my personal voice, not just one you can hear but one that only I have control of (inner jenner). This leadership voice has begun to blossom again into its confidence and believe once again that I am worth hearing. My journey is not nearly over, but I would not be anywhere close to the point I am at now without Dr. K's amazing teachings and the outstanding support. I have my voice, and proud to say, "Hear me ROAR!"

Elizabeth Simmons is a paramedic.

My Voice Victory Take-Away:

_____

_____

_____

_____

_____

My Hope For You...

A portion of the lyrics from Carrie Underwood's hit song, "The Champion" are...

I am invincible, unbreakable
Unstoppable, unshakeable
They knock me down, I get up again
I am the champion
You're gon' know my name
You can't hurt me now
I can't feel the pain
I was made for this, yeah, I was born to win
I am the champion...

These words ring loudly in my spirit like my own personal theme song. These words remind me of the power of my authentic voice to conquer,

146

to overcome, and to win. It doesn't mean that I will never stare defeat in the face. It simply means defeat is not strong enough to render me dysfunctional. I will choose to focus on my victories!

My hope for you is that you have been inspired to celebrate your own voice victories. If you are going to position your authentic voice in a way that allows you to harness your power and master your influence, then you should commit to celebrating every voice win you have. After all, if you don't celebrate your voice, you shouldn't expect anyone else to do it.

TAKE YOUR POSITION!

Celebrating your voice is the foundation for voice victory. Before you proceed to the next section of the book, you must take your position:

1. **Stand in Your Authentic Voice** – Celebrate! You've got this!
2. **Harness Your Power** – Celebrate! You've got this!
3. **Master Your Influence** – Celebrate! You've got this!

MY VOICE COMMITMENT LETTER

Dear _____

Today, I commit to:

_____

_____

_____

_____

_____

_____

_____

_____

_____

Love,

_____

Amplifying the Voices of Others (Voice Freedom)

Amplifying the Voice of Others (Voice Freedom)

When you powerfully position your voice, you are then empowered to amplify the voices of others. ~Dr. K

In a heart-to-heart conversation with a young woman, she said something that grabbed my heart: "Dr. K, when someone makes you invisible or chooses not to hear you, that SILENCE is so very loud."

As I reflected on her words, I thought about how hurtful and harmful it is to intentionally make others invisible when they are perceived as insignificant, less than, or inferior. I thought about the heartache associated with intentionally ignoring a person because it is believed what they have to say is not valuable. I thought about the trauma to a person's soul when their presence in a room is disregarded. My heart broke for this powerful young woman, whose truest desire was simply to be seen, to be heard, and to be valued.

From The Research
Embedded within a research study participant's expressions were feelings of resentment as she shared, "I did speak up. I just wasn't recognized, heard, or acknowledged. I literally

> spoke, so I had a voice, but I had no power. I didn't have any influence. They want me to speak up, but my words are not seen as valuable.

These and other voice experiences like these, is one of the reasons I wrote this book. My own experiences, coupled with the experiences of others, created within me a deep desire to lift the voices of other women.

It wasn't that I wanted us to be louder, I wanted our sound to be lifted. I wanted our authentic voice narratives to be expanded. I wanted our authentic voices increased in power and strengthened for influence.

I wanted us to know the path to our freedom and that the freedom of others is linked to the way in which we masterfully position our voices. I wanted us to be amplifiers in the world – for ourselves and for every other woman who needs to be amplified. That's what I wanted.

Although I wanted these things, I also recognized there really is no voice utopia. There are barriers and there are opportunities. In order to make strides toward this ideal, we must consider some specific *voice* dynamics involved.

Competing Voices (comparison and jealousy)

Do women really compete with each other? Do women really compare themselves to others? Are women really jealous of each other?

The answer to these questions is, NO! All women do not compete, do not compare, and are not jealous. Are there some that are? Absolutely, there are. However, that is not where we you need to focus your attention. Why? Your voice is amplified when you align it with those who are not afraid to let yours shine!

The world is filled with an abundance of women who would love nothing more than to see you win, see you soar, and see your authentic voice amplified. That is where I want you to focus your attention. It requires too much of your energy to keep your eyes on those who may not support you, lift you, push you, or promote you.

Now is the time to silence the competing voices in your life. Do not fight for the spotlight. The stage is big enough for all of us. More importantly, don't even jump on the stage until you know it is your time.

Don't make moves because everyone else is doing it, or because you tell yourself you should. "Shoulds" can cause you to become misaligned with your authenticity and take you down paths that were never yours to travel.

Instead of feeling the competition or being triggered by it, use competition as fuel to establish a standard for positioning your voice. Don't make it about undermining, backstabbing, and one-upping. Make it about stepping up and bringing others along with you.

It takes nothing from you to elevate others. In fact, it adds greatly to your life and legacy. Trying to diminish the light of others to make yours seem brighter puts your light out completely. Instead, keep your light and allow it to light the way for your authentic voice. Otherwise, you'll wander aimlessly in your own darkness.

Voice Action: There will be opportunities to get distracted by competing voices. However, you have the power to influence these situations in a positive way. *When you are faced with these challenges, what will you do? (Hint: Posting about it on Social Media is not an option)*

_____

_____

_____

_____

_____

Collaborative Voices

There is great power in collaboration because "our voices" are stronger together! When we worry about who will get the credit, whose name will be first, and who will own it, we talk ourselves out of the collective power that comes with joining our voice with others. Yes...solos are good. But, perhaps there are times when you should consider singing with the choir.

I worked for nearly ten years in a philanthropic organization that provided grant funding for nonprofit organizations. In many of the conversations with grant recipients, they talked about their challenges with collaborating with other organizations because many of them did not know how to play nicely in the sandbox together. If they could not make the rules of the game, they did not want to play.

But, the truth of the matter is we are so much better together. My husband says it this way, "Things go better together. If you only have two teeth, they work better ... together."

Collaboration is a tremendous opportunity to amplify the voices of others. Joining gifts, talents, abilities, and resources together builds the capacity for greater impact. It is the ultimate amplification because synergistic alliances have a way of turning up the volume so things that need to be heard, can be heard.

I have had the privilege to provide consulting to a phenomenal organization in South Carolina, the Women's Rights and Empowerment Network (WREN). WREN's work is focused on building a movement to advance the health, economic well-being, and rights of women and girls by providing a strong collective voice around the issues that matter most. This work happens through collaborative partnerships. Together, they have been able to advocate, educate, empower, and build coalitions through speaking out and leading the way toward positive change and changing the landscape for women and girls in the state. In fact, WREN and its collaborative partners created an entire campaign and program entitled, "Seen and Heard" - aimed at elevating the stories of women and gender minorities to create conversation and awareness around shared opportunities and barriers.

I shared this example to highlight the fact that powerful innovation and transformation happens when we are intentional to amplify together. Yes. There are voices that work against togetherness. They are divisive and destructive. However, powerfully positioning your authentic voice creates an opportunity for you to model a different way. Don't step away from the opportunity. Instead, step into it.

Historically, the women and men that led significant change in the world stepped into the opportunities to lead change and they were smart enough to know they could not do it alone. Any real movement, any real change, any significant transformation happened through collaborative voices committed to amplifying the voices of the collective.

I challenge you to bring others alongside you in your efforts. Whether you have to reach back, or reach forward, or reach across, come together with others for the purpose of amplification. The power and influence you will have will be your fuel for change and transformation for those who may not be heard unless you help to turn up their volume.

Voice Action: There will be opportunities to collaborate with others for the purpose of amplifying voices. *When you are faced with these opportunities, what will you do? How will you do it?*

_____

_____

_____

_____

_____

_____

Connecting Voices (passing them the mic)

I was facilitating a session on Inclusive Excellence for HERS Leadership Institute. HERS creates and sustains a diverse community of women leaders through leadership development programs and other strategies, with a special focus on gender equity and excellence in higher education.

One of the participants in the session asked about the effectiveness of mentoring for emerging leaders in higher education. I responded by sharing with her that while having a mentor is a wonderful resource, she also needed a sponsor. I shared with her the difference. A mentor is your teacher, your confidant, and your cheerleader. A sponsor is the person who has access to where you want to go, and they hold the door open for you to enter in. In other words, a mentor teaches you how to act when you get to the table. A sponsor invites you to the table and makes sure you have a seat.

I have been blessed with amazing mentors and sponsors on my journey. In fact, I am certain my path would have been very different without some critical interventions and interjections from mentors and sponsors. That is the power of connecting voices. They have been intentional in helping me make connections and/or making connections for me.

What is most powerful is that there have been times when they could have taken great opportunities for themselves. Instead, they gave those opportunities to me. They passed me the mic. They made space for my authentic voice.

I have stood on stages where they could have stood, but they passed the mic to me. I have gotten clients they could have had, but they passed the mic to me. I have gotten credit they could have gotten, but they passed the mic to me. Why? It was important to them to connect me, like others in their journey had once done for them.

Some would call these actions "paying it forward" – I call these actions passing the mic. In other words, they put something in my hand to allow my authentic voice to be amplified. Likewise, because I believe, to whom much is given, much is required, I have made it my mission to pass the mic to others.

I often talk to leaders about their leadership legacy. What will others remember about you when you are no longer here? What will others say about you when you are gone? What do you want them to remember and say? For me, I want to be known for passing the mic. I want others to know that I had a deep desire to make sure their voices were amplified.

When I write, when I teach, when I coach, when I speak, or when I consult, I am passing the mic. I am giving whatever I have to give in an effort to turn up the volume of others.

Voice Action: In a society where mindsets of "Me" and "Mine" are the focus, you have a tremendous opportunity to open the way for others by passing them the mic. It takes absolutely nothing from us to give to others in this way. In fact, it enlarges our territory because once we have passed the mic to them wherever they are they take us into those spaces with them. I have literally been standing on stages where I knew I was also standing on the shoulders of those who passed the mic to me, so I could be there. Who are those in your sphere of influence that you need to pass the mic to?

_____

_____

_____

_____

_____

_____

Freedom

We know we have reached a place of freedom when we position our authentic voice to amplify the voices of others. This is the epitome of your voice journey. You see, standing in your authentic voice is never just about you. Harnessing your power is never just about you. Mastering your influence is never just about you. Others are always connected to our journey, even when we don't see them, even when we don't know they are there. Nevertheless, when we position our authentic voice in powerful ways and we model the way for others, freedom comes to us all.

My Hope For You…

I believe you have committed to doing the work. I believe you are ready. I believe you have the power. I believe you have the influence. I believe in you. My hope for you is that you believe it too. I hope by now you know the "stuff" you're made of.

I hope you know your authentic voice so well that you are no longer afraid to tell your voice story. I hope you trust your authentic voice to the degree you will confidently go in the direction it leads you. I hope you will create space for your authentic voice, because it not only needs to be heard, it needs to be seen. I hope you will protect your authentic voice and secure it against those things that would seek to harm or destroy it. I hope you will nurture and care for your voice so that I will be in good health and prosper. I hope that you will celebrate your voice victories and the voice victories of others along your journey. And finally, I hope your will find freedom in amplifying the voices of others.

TAKE YOUR POSITION!

YOU'VE GOT THIS!

MY VOICE COMMITMENT LETTER

Dear _____

Today, I commit to:

_____

_____

_____

_____

_____

_____

_____

_____

_____

Love,

_____

Finally... In Honor

Through sharing their perceptions and experiences of silence in the workplace and assigning meaning and sense-making to their individual journeys, each of the women in my research study were able to honor and validate their journeys and to embrace some aspect of personal power through telling their stories.

For five of the participants, though not pleasant to revisit, the interview process empowered them to delve deeply into their secrets of silence and to expose elements of oppression or oppressive behaviors enacted through their silence.

For two of the participants who entered the interview process with a strong sense of voice, reflecting on instances of silence seemed to further catalyze their desire to sustain their voices.

For one participant, her journey in silence propelled a deep desire for a journey out of silence. Thus, with experiences of silence and voice in the same organization, sharing her lived experiences in the interview process offered a greater sense of emancipation of voice.

I honor each of the eight research participants for their authentic truth-telling. They were the spark that ignited the fire in my belly to want to help women position their voices in ways that allows them to harness their power and master their influence.

I honor them for their bravery. I honor them for their journeys. I honor them for their voice. Without them, I would not have been able to hear what I desperately needed to hear... The Power of Authentic Voice!

Not... The End
The Beginning

EPILOGUE

For almost a decade now, I have been on my journey to spiritual and emotional wholeness. It has taken me from counselors, to small groups, to therapists, clergy, accountability partners, workshops, you name it. I have been doing the work, ready to face the world healthy and whole. Isn't that what we all strive for?; To be the best version of who God has created us to be despite our detours, our pasts, our regrets, our failures, and at times, our inability to see that we are even worth the fight. Throughout those years, I learned to love myself, forgive myself and others, to set boundaries not only for myself, but others. I learned to have confidence in myself and assert myself, and slowly but surely, I was changing into who I always knew I could be. I was "healed", I was "whole". Or was I?

I believed I was. However, every now and then there were instances where I didn't know what to say, how to respond, or how to speak up, especially in difficult conversations. Instead of exploring those feeling as I was taught to do so, I swept them under the rug and rationalized them away with the adage of "sometimes you just need to be quiet", or "this is not the right time". I was comfortable with that, it was non-threatening, and I was still whole, right? Wrong!

I learned I was wrong because along came Dr. Katrina Hutchins. I met Dr. K through her sister Lady Kristie Searcy who mentioned we should talk because we had some things in common and she thought my "little book" was a great read. During our first phone conversation, she blew my mind with one small statement. As we were conversing on a myriad of topics, she mentioned the importance of using your voice. She said, I'm paraphrasing. "The enemy tries to take our voice as early as he can. After his conversation with Eve in the Garden of Eden and he lies to her, we never hear Eve's voice again".

I wanted to scream, I never considered the impact of my voice. The mere fact that Satan himself wants to destroy it should let us know how powerful it could be, it should be... if only it wasn't snatched from us at some point. Prior to our conversation, I had never considered that my journey now needed to include regaining my voice. But how would I do that? When and where did I lose it? How did I lose it? What happened? And so my new journey began. When Dr. Hutchins shared that she was writing a new book dedicated to voice, I was elated at the possibility of using it as part of my journey. The Voice Positioning System has allowed me to see myself in an entire different light. I realized that I am my voice, and I had to learn to own it, to know it, to trust it, to create a space for its authenticity, to protect it the same way I protect my mind and my heart, to nurture it, celebrate it, and most importantly, amplify the voices of beautiful women around me that I have the privilege to speak life into day after day.

The same way the GPS in our car gives us the directions to our destinations, so will the VPS give you the direction of your life. The Voice Positioning System has taught me that to live a spiritually and emotionally whole life, I need my voice – my authentic, bold, fearless and steadfast voice.

No matter where you might find yourself right now, recognize that you may have done all the work you think is required, but I would beseech you to take another look. You may have read through the book cover to cover and skipped the work altogether. You may have just highlighted a few good nuggets. You may have started some exercises but couldn't complete them. If this is you, I ask you to go back and do the work required in each chapter. Dig deep. Do the work. I promise if you take the time, you will find your authentic voice and walk in such a way that your light will never be dimmed again.

This book was not written overnight. It was written over a lifetime worth of experiences. And in that same manner, will now take you a lifetime to master it. Allow it to be a part of your daily tool kit. This is your time to TAKE YOUR POSITION, Reclaim Your Authentic Voice, Harness Your Power and Master Your Influence.

Thank you Dr. K: Your work has allowed me to find my authentic voice, a journey that I will share in my continuous voyage of CHANGE and realize that my voice is not just an expression of my words, it an expression of who I am.

Lady Charlet Lewis
Author of *I Had to Change – Conquering My Past To Embrace My Future*
www.LadyCharlet.com

GRATITUDE

Long before I knew it, this book was already in the making. I have my second-grade teacher and a little boy in my class to thank for that.

Special thanks to my editor, Dr. Kristie Searcy at *Class A Editing*. You were the first to see the words on these pages and to respond back to me regarding what you saw. Your feedback was invaluable and your trusted voice, powerful.

It takes a special gift to turn someone's words into something that is graphically beautiful. Thank you, Andria Cox for contributing to this work in such a meaningful way.

Much of the personal journey I shared on the pages of this book, I lived out with the people who mean more to me than any other earthly possession – my family. I remain grateful for how you support and love me always. Special thank you to my sissy, Kimberly Jowers. Having you sit at the kitchen table and to through some of these concepts was priceless. I appreciate you!

To the love of my life, Bishop Derrick W. Hutchins, Sr, I don't have enough space to write it all here. So, I'll just say – Thank you for everything, Babe! Just… Thank You! #HutchLove

Above all else, I am grateful to God for the gift of my Authentic Voice.

ABOUT DR. K

Dr. Katrina (formerly Spigner) Hutchins, affectionately known as, "Dr. K" is the President & CEO of Re-Source Solutions, LLC, a personal and professional growth and development company. A Certified Personal & Executive Coach, Consultant, Inspirational Speaker, Author, and Assistant Professor with decades of experience as a senior leader in the nonprofit, philanthropic, and higher education sectors, Dr. K is committed to positioning her voice in a way that amplifies the voices of others. As such, she has coached individuals and spoken to audiences all over the country.

Whether in auditoriums, one-on-one, through radio, television, in the board room, in the classroom, or in whatever space she finds herself, Dr. K's goal remains the same – to touch the lives and work of others and to leave them better than before.

Dr. K earned a Bachelor of Arts degree from Columbia College and a Master's degree in Social Work from the University of South Carolina. She also earned a certificate in Clinical Pastoral Education. Additionally, she earned her Certification in Personal & Executive coaching from the Coaching and Positive Psychology Institute (CaPP). Dr. K earned her Doctoral degree in Education with a concentration in Organizational Leadership from Northeastern University. Dr.K's research is focused on the power of women's voices.

Dr. K is also the author of three inspirational books: *This Is for You!: 31 Days of Life-Changing Discoveries, G.I.F.T.: Growing In Faith*

Today!, and her most recent book, *COUNTERFEIT: Lies That Cover the Naked Truth.*

Dr. K's mantra for her life is "Life happens...Put on your Big Girl Panties and keep moving!" Learn more about Dr. K and her work at her company site, www.re-sourcesolutions.com.

WORKS CONSULTED

1. (Morrison & Milliken, 2000; Milliken & Morrison, 2003; Morrison & Milliken, 2003; Perlow & Williams, 2003).
2. (Zerubavel, 2006)